The French Imparfait and
Passé Simple in Discourse

Summer Institute of Linguistics and
The University of Texas at Arlington
Publications in Linguistics

Publication 116

Editors

Donald A. Burquest
University of Texas
at Arlington

William R. Merrifield
Summer Institute of
Linguistics

Assistant Editors

Rhonda L. Hartell

Marilyn A. Mayers

Consulting Editors

Doris A. Bartholomew
Pamela M. Bendor-Samuel
Desmond C. Derbyshire
Robert A. Dooley
Jerold A. Edmondson

Austin Hale
Robert E. Longacre
Eugene E. Loos
Kenneth L. Pike
Viola G. Waterhouse

The French Imparfait and Passé Simple in Discourse

Sharon Rebecca Rand

A Publication of
The Summer Institute of Linguistics
and
The University of Texas at Arlington
1993

© 1993 by the Summer Institute of Linguistics, Inc.

Library of Congress Catalog No: 93–60371

ISBN: 0–88312–822–5

ISSN: 1040–0850

Cover sketch and design by Hazel Shorey

Copies of this and other publications of the Summer Institute of Linguistics may be obtained from

International Academic Bookstore
7500 W. Camp Wisdom Road
Dallas, TX 75236

Contents

List of Abbreviations

COND	conditional	PRSPCPL	present participle
FUT	future	PRSSBJ	present subjunctive
IMP	imparfait	PS	passé simple
IMPSBJ	imperfect subjunctive	PSTPCPL	past participle
INF	infinitive	S	sentence
INTJ	interjection	1	first-person
NEG	negative	2	second-person
PA	passé antérieur	3	third-person
PART	partitive	s	singular
PC	passé composé	p	plural
PQP	plus-que-parfait	?	meaning unknown
PRES/PRS	present	/	line division in examples from poetry

Acknowledgments

I would first like to thank Dr. Robert Longacre for his patience and open-mindedness in guiding me through the writing of this study. I also express my appreciation to Dr. John Stuart for his encouragement and his patient reading of various drafts, and to Dr. Shin Ja Hwang for her corrections and helpful suggestions.

I express my thanks as well to Mark Bostrom for countless discussions which sharpened my focus and helped me to relate the contributions of various authors to the data. His insights, suggestions, and encouragement greatly improved the content of this paper, and his skills in editing and formatting greatly improved its appearance.

I wish to thank also the many friends and family members who have encouraged me and prayed for me over the long process of research and writing. Special appreciation is due to my three roommates: Sue McLain, Lucy Spiro, and Charlene Persons for their patience and good humor.

Editions Gallimard of Paris has kindly authorized the reproduction of text from their 1943 booklet *Le Passe—Muraille* by Marcel Aymé, which formed the central part of the corpus upon which this study is based and which appears in the appendix in interlinearized format. I am most grateful.

Above all, I lift my gratitude to God, who gives strength and encouragement without measure.

1
The Imparfait and the Passé Simple: Different Approaches

One does not have to read much French narrative to realize the importance of the passé simple and imparfait alternation in this genre. These two tenses dominate French literary narrative.

Of the two, the imparfait seems the more difficult to define. Aside from its occurrence outside the narrative genre, it seems to have a wide variety of uses, sometimes even taking the place of the passé simple as the tense of narration. Various definitions have been put forward to explain its use. Such definitions usually attempt to define the tense in terms of the qualities that characterize its usage in isolated sentences, and these tend to be followed by pages of examples of particular uses of the imparfait, many of which do not seem to be related.

On the other hand, some authors have very convincingly argued that the imparfait/passé simple opposition plays an important role at the level of discourse structure. The primary function assigned to it here does not appear to have an immediate connection with the temporal values which have been associated with the two tenses at a sentence level.

The premise of this book is that the imparfait and the passé simple each have a basic meaning that underlies their discourse functions. An attempt is made to propose a characterization of the imparfait that connects these two levels of function, one which can be as clearly seen in the dynamics of an entire text as in individual sentences. With the understanding that it is difficult to define the use of either the imparfait or the passé simple in isolation and that the two are usually seen as occupying opposing values, they are defined together, as complementary entities. The characterization of the imparfait is then shown to account for stylistic uses of the imparfait as well as for the classical passé simple/imparfait opposition.

1

French has five past tenses: the passé composé, the passé simple, the imparfait, the plus-que-parfait, and the passé antérieur. The way in which any of these is translated into English may vary, depending on the context; however, a general description of these tenses can be given in terms of their English equivalents. The plus-que-parfait and the less common passé antérieur correspond to the English pluperfect. The passé composé corresponds both to the English past tense (*I went*) and to the English past perfect tense (*I have gone*). The passé simple is only used in written narrative and it also corresponds to the English past tense.

As the imparfait is the focus of this paper, its functions are described in detail later. For a beginning, we note that it encompasses all of the aspects that Comrie categorizes as "imperfective": (1) the continuous-progressive, (2) the continuous-nonprogressive, and (3) the habitual (1976:25). Examples of these would be (1) *Tom was going*, (2) *Tom was standing by the chair*, and (3) *Tom used to go to church*.

The purpose of this study is to analyze the uses of the imparfait and the passé simple tenses in French literary narrative, and to propose a characterization of the passé simple as event and the imparfait as state.

This chapter examines traditional and recent characterizations of the imparfait and the passé simple. Chapter two sets forth one quality of the imparfait, nonboundedness, as a core value that ties together the other important characteristics associated with the imparfait. The opposing trait of boundedness will be shown to characterize the passé simple. Chapter three introduces the concepts of event and state, defined in terms of boundedness and nonboundedness. Event and state as communicational concepts are further modified in terms of the author's perceptions and communicational intent. Chapter four explores the relationship between verb or predicate types and the imparfait and the passé simple.

Chapter five examines specific uses of the imparfait that have been listed by grammarians and shows how these, as well as the uses of the passé simple, can be accounted for by the definitions of event and state. Finally, chapter six demonstrates how the event/state opposition functions in a narrative text as a whole.

Some of the questions that initially motivated this study of the imparfait were:

1.   How does an author decide whether to use the imparfait or the passé simple in a given sentence?
2.   To what extent can these tenses be used in ways that seem to contradict their primary uses? For example, can the imparfait be used to narrate a story? Can the passé simple be used to give

description? What differing effects can be achieved by using them in these ways?

3. Are there verbs or constructions that can take only the imparfait or only the passé simple?

This study is limited to dealing with the imparfait only as it is found in the genre of literary narrative. Although it is recognized that the imparfait alternates with the passé composé in spoken French in essentially the same way that it alternates with the passé simple in written narrative texts, the focus of this study is the imparfait/passé simple opposition. Some relevant examples of the imparfait/passé composé opposition are, however, examined. The study does not deal with the so-called modal uses of the imparfait; these are considered secondary to its temporal/aspectual uses. It treats the imparfait only where it has past-time, nonhypothetical meaning. Finally, it does not treat the changes of the imparfait over time; the focus is on the uses of the imparfait current today.

A clear characterization of the imparfait would have implications for (1) text analysis and translation, as well as (2) the teaching of French to nonnative speakers.

1.1–1.6 Grammatical approaches

1.1. *Grammaire Larousse*. The Larousse grammar of French (*Grammaire Larousse* 1964:341) defines the imparfait in the following way:

> It is a past tense of simple form: it is capable of translating **incomplete action** (incomplete aspect). It is perfectly suited to the expression of the **duration** of an action, and **it marks neither the beginning nor the end of this action.**[1]

This well-known grammar goes on to define three main temporal uses of imparfait constructions: (1) to describe the circumstances that existed before an action recounted in the passé simple; (2) to comment on a fact reported in the passé simple; (3) to underline the importance of previous events. (p. 341)

The passé simple, on the other hand, is defined in terms of the recounting of past events. (p. 346)

---

[1]All translation from the French sources are the author's unless otherwise specified. Also, throughout this volume, boldface type is used by the author in both quotations and examples to focus attention on the items under discussion.

1.2. Grévisse. In *Le Bon Usage*, Grévisse (1980:833) gives the following characterization of the imparfait:

> The imparfait indicates, under the durative aspect, that of **continuity** (like a process line), **an action** that was still **incomplete** ... at the moment the subject was speaking; it shows this action in the process of occurring in **duration**, excluding it from present occurrences and **without showing either its initial or final phase**.

He explains the function of the passé simple in the following way:

> The *passé simple* (*passé défini*) expresses an action that was completely accomplished at a particular moment in the past, without consideration of the contact that this action, in itself or through its circumstances, might have with the present. Of itself, it implies neither the idea of continuity nor that of simultaneity in relation to a past action; it marks an action-point. (1980:837)

1.3. Imbs. A third grammarian, Paul Imbs (1960:90), gives yet another definition of the imparfait:

> This "tense" ... has ... great suggestive force in the extent to which it expresses **the continuous time** (indefinite **duration**) upon which our intelligence carves out the discontinuous moments in which events occur. The essential characteristic of this continuity is that, **in itself, it has neither beginning nor end**, unless its term is indicated by the context; actually, neither the beginning of the process nor the end are of interest to the imparfait as such. All the specific uses [of the imparfait] can be explained on the basis of this fundamental value.

Imbs' view of the passé simple is as follows:

> The passé simple represents an event **seen from the outside**, in its globality impenetrable to analysis. It does not exclude duration but it treats it as an abstraction which it is ready to express by lexical means. It is thus perfectly correct to say: "The meeting **lasted** [PS] two hours" if the action reported is in a series of other events seen in their succession and not in the internal duration of each. (1960:86)

Although these definitions are not identical, there does seem to be agreement on four particular characteristics of the imparfait: continuity, duration, uncompleted action, and lack of reference to either the beginning or the end of the situation it encodes. According to these authors, then, these four qualities would appear to be the essential characteristics of the imparfait.

This traditional approach, which gives a list of traits that may or may not be relevant to a given usage of the imparfait or the passé simple, has failed to satisfy many. One group that has found it particularly frustrating has been teachers of French. A number have attempted to find a more straightforward explanation of the distinction between these tenses.

1.4. Abrate. Abrate is one who finds some of the traditional conceptions of the imparfait (or imperfect) to be inadequate. Although she is concerned with the imparfait as it occurs in opposition to the passé composé, the solution that she proposes seems applicable also to the imparfait as it alternates with the passé simple.

Abrate (1983:549) characterizes the passé composé as expressing "termination or momentariness," while the imparfait expresses "continuity or repetition." She further notes that verbs that are "momentary" tend to occur in the passé composé and verbs that are "nonmomentary" in the imparfait. However, she admits that this tendency is not absolute and proposes a hypothesis of focus or emphasis to account for these cases. Her formula (p. 548) is shown in (1).

(1)   Abrate's emphasis model

	Momentary verbs	Nonmomentary verbs
Imperfect	continuity or repetition emphasized	without contrary indications
Passé composé	without contrary indications	termination or momentariness emphasized

By "contrary indications," she seems to be referring mostly to contextual factors such as temporal markers (e.g., *toujours*), which may be "explicit or understood." The passé composé is thus the default tense for momentary verbs, and the imparfait the default tense for nonmomentary verbs.

1.5. Cox. Another who approaches the problem from a pedagogical point of view is Thomas Cox. Although Cox does not reject characterizations such as "uncompleted" versus "completed," he finds them "not effective" as a means of teaching the opposition to English speakers

(1982:231). According to Cox, English speakers consider all past tenses as completive, and thus do not understand this type of contrast.

Cox does find one aspectual distinction that he considers effective: inceptive (or inchoative) versus noninceptive (noninchoative). He claims that the passé composé is always inceptive (i.e., includes the beginning of an action) while the imparfait is always noninceptive (i.e., excludes the beginning of an action). He (1982:231) gives the examples in (2) to illustrate this distinction.

(2)   *Il m'a fallu* [PC] *deux heures pour préparer ce repas.*
        Il me fallait [IMP] *deux heures pour préparer ce repas.*

Although the difference between these sentences is difficult to translate into English, the first might be equivalent to *It took me two hours to prepare this meal,* while the second could not be translated this way. However, both might be read as *I needed two hours to prepare this meal.* The difference is that the first sentence indicates that the action in question did take place while the second does not carry this information. Cox (1982:232) defines the imparfait as lacking a "well-defined temporal limit at its forward edge," a view that he attributes to Grobe (1967). According to Cox, it is this forward edge that distinguishes the passé composé action as one that actually did take place.

Another pair of examples which Cox gives is:

(3)   *Il se noyait* [IMP].   He was drowning.
        Il s'est noyé [PC].   He drowned.

Cox (1982:233) argues that the important difference between these two sentences is that the first "excludes the beginning from the speaker's focus whereas [the second] describes the action from its inception." Cox asserts that this distinction holds for all verbs, even those considered terminative in meaning.

1.6. Comrie. Still another who objects to a number of traditional characterizations of the imparfait and passé simple is Bernard Comrie. Comrie's interest is not just in the imparfait and passé simple but in a universal definition of the qualities that distinguish these two tenses, as well as similarly opposed tenses in other languages. The terms that Comrie is seeking to define are perfectivity, which would be the defining characteristic of the passé simple and passé composé, and imperfectivity, which would be the defining characteristic of the imparfait.

His work (*Aspect* 1976) attempts to disprove a number of traditional characterizations of perfectivity and imperfectivity. As we have seen, duration is one quality that has been used in this way. Comrie (1976:16) notes that duration is often used to distinguish a perfective, which is said to indicate short duration, from an imperfective, which would indicate long duration.

To refute this definition, Comrie (1976:17) gives the example of the two French sentences in (4). He translates both as 'he reigned thirty years'. Since both are perfectly grammatical in French and both express the same duration of time, the idea of a time boundary that would separate the two tenses is seen to be false.

(4)   *Il régna* [PS] *trente ans.*
       Il régnait [IMP] *trente ans.*

Comrie also discards the theory that the perfective applies to a situation with "limited, as opposed to unlimited duration." He points out that "thirty years, an hour, ten years . . . are all limited periods," but, as his examples show, "both perfective and imperfective forms can be used to describe such duration" (p. 17). These examples also serve to disprove a "characterization [of perfectivity] as indicating a punctual (i.e., point-like) or momentary situation" (p. 17).

Another hypothesis that Comrie rejects is that perfectivity "indicates a completed action." His quarrel here is with the word "completed." He feels that the perfective "puts no more emphasis, necessarily, on the end of the situation than on any other part," representing all parts of the situation as a "single whole" (p. 18).

Having dealt with these common, but in his view, inadequate approaches, Comrie proposes his own definitions: perfectivity "involves lack of explicit reference to the internal temporal constituency of a situation" (p. 20), while imperfectivity must be characterized by "explicit reference to the internal temporal constituency of a situation" (p. 24). Thus, where perfective aspect is used, the situation is viewed externally—as a "blob" (p. 18); where imperfective aspect occurs, the situation is viewed internally.

1.7–1.8 Discourse approaches

Another and distinctly different way of viewing the passé simple/imparfait distinction is represented by the theories developed through text analysis. Whereas the authors we have looked at thus far have been willing to deal with distinctions on the basis of one or two sentences, proponents of textlinguistics consider the individual sentence to be incomplete in itself as a unit of analysis and insist that grammatical forms such as verb tenses have discourse level functions that must be taken into account.

1.7. Strong focus versus weak focus. Reid takes such an approach, viewing the defining value of the imparfait/passé simple opposition as "emphasis on the event named by the verb." His claim is that the passé simple signals "strong concentration of attention on the event" while the imparfait signals "weak concentration of attention on the event" (1977:315).

Reid sees this distinction as comparable to the difference in English between the phrases *that* book and *the* book and thus views the passé simple and the imparfait as types of "verbal deictics" (p. 315). As a demonstration of this type of focus, Reid gives the example in (5) taken from *Un coeur simple,* a short story by Gustave Flaubert (1965:150).

(5) *Pendant un demi-siècle les bourgeoises de Pont-l'Evêque envièrent à Mme. Aubain sa servante Félicité.*

Pour cent francs par an, elle faisait la cuisine et le ménage, cousait, lavait, repassait, savait brider un cheval, engraisser les volailles, battre le beurre, et resta fidèle à sa maîtresse,—qui cependant n'était pas une personne agréable.

For half a century the middle class women of Pont-l'Evêque envied Mme. Aubain her servant Félicité.

For one hundred francs a year, she **did** [IMP] the cooking and the housecleaning, **sewed** [IMP], **washed** [IMP], **ironed** [IMP], **knew** [IMP] how to bridle a horse, fatten chickens, churn butter and **remained** [PS] faithful to her mistress—who was not, however, easy to get along with.

Reid's contention is that the final verb in this series, *resta,* is put into the passé simple because it is the one in focus. The story concerns the character of the main participant, Félicité, and thus her trait of faithfulness to her mistress is emphasized while her more mundane activities are rendered in the low-focus imparfait.

To avoid basing his claim on the subjective types of arguments which he feels too often characterize treatments of the imparfait, Reid supports his statements with statistical data showing significant correlations between the passé simple and such phenomena as nonstative verbs, affirmative constructions, independent clauses, human subjects, first-person subjects, singular subjects, subjects referred to by a proper name, and central (story) characters.[2] The imparfait, on the other hand, shows itself to be associated with the opposing values of stative verb être, negation, relative clauses, inanimate subjects, third-person subjects, plural subjects, pronoun subjects, and peripheral characters. His reasoning for selecting each of these variables is a "perceptual bias" which seems to link it with a high-focus or a low-focus situation.

1.8. Foregrounding versus backgrounding. A similar view of the passé simple/imparfait distinction is that of foregrounding versus backgrounding, another framework developed through text analysis. Weinrich (1989) was one of the first exponents of this view. He speaks of a RELIEF TEMPOREL composed of a foreground (*premier plan*) and a background (*arrière-plan*). Into the former, he groups the passé simple and passé antérieur tenses, while the latter consists of the imparfait and plus-que-parfait tenses. His passé simple/imparfait distinction is that of RHEME (*focalisation*) versus THEME (*topicalisation*) (1989:129).

The influence of both Weinrich and Reid can be seen in the work of Hopper, who makes a number of far-reaching claims. Citing Reid's statistics, Hopper (1979b) identifies Reid's high-focus versus low-focus opposition of the passé simple and the imparfait with his own foregrounding/backgrounding distinction. He points out that the correlations discovered by Reid correspond to qualities that he himself has found to be associated with perfective and imperfective aspect. Hopper's (1979b:216) perfectivity-imperfectivity chart in (6) shows these qualities.

Hopper (1979b:39) claims that passé simple sentences are characterized by chronological sequencing such that "the beginning of one event is contingent upon the completion of the preceding event" (p. 58). This contingency, in his view, is the ground "from [which] ... the notion of completeness which is characteristic of perfective aspect derives ... " He equates this "notion of completeness" with "the idea of the action viewed as a whole" (p. 58).

---

[2]In Reid's sample of 689 verbs, the verb être accounts for 11.9 percent of imparfait forms as opposed to only 1.3 percent of passé simple forms. Of all imparfait forms, 14.3 percent are negated, while only 1.7 percent of passé simple forms are negated. Human subjects occur with about 95.5 percent of passé simple forms as opposed to 79.5 percent of imparfait forms, and the first person occurs with 78.4 percent of passé simple forms as opposed to 62 percent of imparfait forms. Singular subjects account for 83.8 percent of passé simple forms as opposed to 66.3 percent of imparfait forms, and central character subjects account for 93.6 percent of passé simple forms as opposed to 78.9 percent of imparfait forms. In relative clauses, 24.3 percent of imparfait forms were found while only 3.7 percent of passé simple forms were found. Finally, 24.1 percent of passé simple forms had a proper noun rather than a pronoun as subject, while only 11.3 percent of imparfait forms had a proper noun subject.

(6)   Hopper's comparison of perfective and imperfective aspect

PERFECTIVE	IMPERFECTIVE
Chronological sequencing	Simultaneity or chronological overlapping of situation C with event A and/or B
View of event as a whole, whose completion is a necessary prerequisite to a subsequent event	View of a situation or happening whose completion is not a necessary prerequisite to a subsequent event
Identity of subject within each discrete episode	Frequent changes of subject
Unmarked distribution of focus in clause, with presupposition of subject and assertion in verb and its immediate complements (or other unmarked focus)	Marked distribution of focus, e.g., subject focus, instrument focus, focus on sentence adverbial
Human topics	Variety of topics, including natural phenomena
Dynamic, kinetic events	Static, descriptive situations
Foregrounding. Event indispensable to narrative	Backgrounding. State or situation necessary for understanding motives, attitudes, etc.
Realis	Irrealis

He notes that imparfait constructions do not have this sequencing characteristic but rather "are permitted to depict events which are simultaneous with those of other sentences or at least in large measure overlapping them" (p. 39). He also observes that these constructions tend to have a wider distribution of topics than passé simple constructions and thus assigns them a "topic-shift" feature.

These observations later became the basis for the Hopper-Thompson Transitivity Hypothesis, which drew the perfective/imperfective distinction together with nine other values of clauses or predicates (presence of an object, kinesis, punctuality, volitionality, affirmation, mode, agency, affectedness of the object, and individuation of the object) into a set of parameters determining the degree of transitivity of a clause (Hopper and Thompson 1980). This hypothesis is not discussed here.

We have thus looked at a number of different approaches to the imparfait and the passé simple and have found that these vary widely. There does not seem to be any common denominator that would allow us to tie them all together.

2
Boundedness and Nonboundedness

2.1. A core semantic value for the imparfait. What is needed is one primary or core value which is always true of the imparfait. This chapter proposes such a core trait and shows that many of the approaches examined can be unified around it. This trait has a corresponding and opposite value which can be seen to characterize the passé simple.

2.2. Boundedness and nonboundedness as core traits. The authors examined up to now and the primary traits that they have attributed to the imparfait can be summarized by the list given in (8). Several of these traits have already been shown not to hold for all uses of the imparfait. For example, duration and incomplete action were both rejected by Comrie for reasons that have already been given.

There are also problems with Cox's inceptive/noninceptive distinction. Although it appears to work for the verbs which he gives as examples, it cannot be said to work, as he claims, for all terminative verbs. For example, the primary distinction between the sentences in (7) is obviously in the completion and not in the inception of the latter.

(7) *Il finissait* [IMP] *son travail.*   He was finishing his work.
 Il a fini [PC] *son travail.*   He finished his work.

Thus from our list of possible defining traits, we can eliminate inceptivity as well as the two traits of continuity and lack of a beginning or an end mentioned by the traditional grammarians in defining the tense.

(8)   Primary traits assigned to the imparfait

	Larousse	Grevisse	Imbs	Abrate	Cox	Comrie	Reid	Weinrich	Hopper
Duration	x	x	x	x					
Uncompleted action	x	x		x					
No beginning or end	x	x	x						
Continuity		x	x	x					
Repetition				x					
Noninchoativity					x				
Focus on internal structure						x			
Low focus							x		
Backgrounding								x	x
Nonsequentiality									x

Imbs (1960:90) has made an interesting statement regarding these qualities:

> [The imparfait] has ... great suggestive force in the extent to which it expresses the continuous time (indefinite duration) upon which our intelligence carves out the discontinuous moments in which events occur. **The essential characteristic of this continuity is that it has neither beginning or end**, unless its term is indicated by the context.

He goes on to make a claim:

> Actually, neither the beginning nor the end of the process are of interest to the imparfait as such. All of the specific uses [of the imparfait] can be explained on the basis of this fundamental value. (1960:90)

Imbs thus claims that the defining characteristic of the imparfait is its lack of beginning or end, or, in other words, of boundaries. This is a claim worth examining.

If we look at the other traits on our list in terms of this quality, some consistencies begin to appear. Continuity, for instance, seems to be redundant: discontinuity implies boundaries of some sort; therefore what has no boundaries is by definition continuous.

That which is unbounded in time is also durative, i.e., has duration. Sten (1952) explains this relationship in a straightforward way. His definitions of the passé simple are given in diagrams: the passé simple is represented as [—] and the imparfait as ([–)—(–]). In his view, the boundaries (represented by the brackets) are the important part of the passé simple; "The middle phase . . . for all practical purposes does not exist" (p. 125).

For the imparfait, on the other hand, the opposite is true. Sten includes the boundaries in his symbolization because he feels that all verbal actions have them, but he puts them in parentheses to show that they are not in focus. "The middle phase . . . is the only one that counts for someone who uses an imparfait" (p. 125). Sten connects this definition to the concept of duration in the following way: "For there to be a middle phase, it is necessary that the action last some time" (p. 127).

If we accept the hypothesis that the primary quality of the imparfait is its lack of boundaries, the basis for a number of other characterizations of the imparfait and passé simple becomes clear. The traditional grammarians, for example, consider the passé simple as terminative and the imparfait as associated with uncompleted action. In other words, they say that the passé simple has a terminative, or final boundary, while the imparfait does not. Cox (1982:232), on the other hand, asserts that the important distinction is that the imparfait is noninceptive, i.e., "lacks a well-defined temporal limit at its forward edge." It "either excludes the beginning or implies that it was already past" (p. 231). It is easy to see that these are both correct but incomplete characterizations of the imparfait.

Comrie's analysis is more complete. He rejects the label of "completed action" for his past perfective in favor of "complete action," thus recognizing the importance of both boundaries. He characterizes the verb in the perfective as a situation seen externally or globally, as a blob or a point. (Imbs also uses this image. See §1.3.) Sten's representation of the passé simple, [—], can easily be reduced to such a blob or point, since the middle phase is, in a practical sense, not there.

As we have seen, Comrie (1976:18) characterizes the imperfective as "explicit reference to the internal temporal constituency of a situation." "Internal temporal constituency" here seems to be the same as Sten's "middle phase" (discussed above).

In a sense, Comrie's "explicit reference to the internal temporal constituency of a situation" and Imb's lack of beginning or end can be seen as two ways of describing the same core value. Comrie's definition is built on the focus that is present in the imparfait and absent in the passé simple, while Imbs has identified the focus that is absent in the imparfait but present in the the passé simple. Thus, the two definitions can be seen as complementary, as two sides of the same coin.

So far, all of these viewpoints seem to fit together. Let us examine another which also seems relevant.

2.3. Boundedness and Grobe's restricted/nonrestricted opposition. Grobe (1967) has set forth his own passé simple/imparfait opposition, based on restrictive versus nonrestrictive aspect. He defines this distinction in the following way:

> If a past action is felt to possess a precise temporal limit at either the one or the other, or both edges of its development, that action is best expressed by the passé simple . . . If a past action is felt to possess no precise temporal limit at the edges of its development, that action is best expressed by the imperfect . . . (Grobe 1967:345)

Grobe thus allows for at least three possibilities in using the passé simple: (1) there will be a boundary at the beginning of the action; (2) there will be a boundary at the end of the action; or (3) there will be a boundary at both the beginning and the end of the action. How does he account for these different possibilities?

For Grobe the answer lies in the perspective or viewpoint of the observer of an action. In his view, the passé simple represents any of these different scenarios: (1) the observer can see the entire action from beginning to end; (2) he is aware only of the beginning boundary or only of the ending boundary of the action; or (3) the action has such short duration that it appears to the observer to have only one single time boundary. Grobe considers all of these situations to have a restrictive aspect (p. 344).

The imparfait, on the other hand, would represent situations that are nonrestrictive. Grobe (1967:344–45) describes three types: (1) the observer arrives on the scene after the beginning or before the end of the action or state. In this way, he does not see the temporal boundary (or boundaries) in question and thus does not have a real awareness of it (or them); (2) an action has such a long duration that its beginning and end are "beyond the horizon of [an observer's] temporal imagination;" (3) an action with definite boundaries "possesses such an absorbing dynamic character that we become more interested in it as pure movement, abstracted from all chronology."

Thus Grobe's approach also recognizes boundaries as the distinction between the imparfait and the passé simple.

2.4. A definition of boundedness. We have been using the terms BOUNDED and NONBOUNDED in rather a loose way up to this point. It might be helpful to examine the meanings that have been associated with these terms in the past in order to understand clearly what is meant, and not meant, by them.

Allen (1966) is credited with the first use of bounded and nonbounded. He uses them to refer to the same properties of a predicate that Garey (1957) designates as TELIC and ATELIC (See §4.3). A bounded proposition in his terms would be one that had a potential goal or end-point, while a nonbounded predication would be one that did not have such an end-point. His boundedness, then, is defined as an inherent quality of the predication and has to do with its having or not having a potential terminal boundary.

Dahl (1981) distinguishes this telic versus atelic property of predications from a second quality, which has also been referred to as telic versus atelic and bounded versus nonbounded. He calls these properties, respectively, the T property and the P property. (Although Dahl does not explain his use of the letters T and P to distinguish these two properties, T would seem to derive from the term telic and P from the term perfective.) Dahl (1981:82) defines his P property as follows: "A situation, process, action, etc. has the P property iff it has the T property and the goal, limit, or terminal point in question is, or is claimed to be, actually reached." He gives the examples in (9) of these two qualities and how they interact.

(9)   not-T   T

   not-P   *I was writing*   *I was writing a letter.*
   P   (does not occur)   *I wrote a letter.*

Dahl's P property does seem to resemble Comrie's perfectivity, in that it is a grammatical category rather than a semantic one. However, it is not the same as the boundaries that Imbs and Sten have mentioned. For one thing, Dahl's quality seems to apply only to terminative boundaries. Secondly, according to Dahl, the P property can only apply to a predication that has the T property.

Now the passé simple can, in theory, be used with any predication and can apply to a terminal boundary or an initial boundary or to both. Therefore, the concept that we want to capture by the idea of BOUNDEDNESS differs from Dahl's T property in that it is ACTUAL rather than potential and COMMUNICATED rather than inherent. It also differs from Dahl's P property in that it (1) can have reference to either a terminal boundary or an initial boundary or both; and (2) can have reference to a predication that is bounded or nonbounded in Allen's sense of the term.

2.5. Boundedness and Abrate's emphasis model. Perhaps the most complex treatment of the imparfait that we examined in chapter one is that of Abrate. Her emphasis, or focus, schema (given earlier in (1)) is set up in a way that is similar to Dahl's chart above (Abrate 1983:548).

(10)

	Momentary verbs	Nonmomentary verbs
Imparfait	Continuity or repetition emphasized	Without contrary indications
Passé composé	Without contrary indications	Termination or momentariness emphasized

Abrate is attempting to explain some characteristics of verb usage in the passé composé and imparfait. She recognizes Reid's and Hopper's observation (see §§1.7–1.8) that some types of verbs seem proper to the passé composé (or passé simple) while others seem proper to the imparfait.

However, as we have noted, it is also true that almost any verb can be used in either the passé composé or the imparfait. Abrate's schema is thus an attempt to clarify this apparent contradiction.

Abrate accounts for these facts by dividing verbs into two categories: momentary and nonmomentary. Momentary verbs would thus naturally occur in the passé composé; the nonmomentary verbs would be most natural to the imparfait.

To explain the fact that momentary verbs sometimes do occur in the imparfait and nonmomentary verbs in the passé composé, Abrate comes up with her emphasis formula, based on the qualities that she considers characteristic of the passé composé and imparfait. She sees these as momentariness or termination for the passé composé and continuity or repetition for the imparfait. If a nonmomentary verb occurs in the passé composé, then the passé simple provides an emphasis on momentariness or termination. If a momentary verb occurs in the imparfait, then the imparfait emphasizes continuity or repetition.

To understand Abrate's categories of momentary and nonmomentary verbs, we should first look at what would distinguish them, one from the other. Abrate (1983:548–9) defines "momentary verbs" in the following way:

> Momentary verbs are those that are normally seen to be definable to a limited "moment" in time and include most action verbs—*parler, aller, voyager, manger, respirer, retourner, prendre, voir*—but also included are verbs such as *durer* and *oublier*, which contain momentary limits implicit in their meanings. It is not necessary to define these limits but to see that they exist.

Abrate thus defines the word "momentary" in terms of "limits," or boundaries. Her nonmomentary verbs, on the other hand, would be those "for which it is more difficult to define the 'moment' of their occurrence" (p. 549), i.e., those that lack definite boundaries.

Assuming that we could represent this boundedness of verb categories as it relates to boundedness of verb tenses, we could make the following chart, which is similar to Dahl's.

(11)   Predicate −B   Predicate +B

     Aspect −B   redundant   marked
     Aspect +B   marked   redundant

Predicate +/−B would cover both Abrate's momentary versus non-momentary verbs and Allen's bounded versus nonbounded predications. This binary category is based on properties of the predication, i.e., the verb with or without an object.

Aspect +B would refer to either the passé simple or the passé composé. Aspect −B would refer to the imparfait. These differ from Dahl's P/non-P in the ways mentioned above.

A chart such as this one explains the affinity of certain predicates for a given aspect. Bounded predications would occur most naturally in a bounded aspect and nonbounded predications in a nonbounded aspect. In other words, it would be most natural for a verb to be redundant in the tense with which it occurs in terms of boundedness.

However, bounded predications do occur in a nonbounded aspect and nonbounded predications do occur in a bounded aspect. We will examine these in more detail in a later chapter, but for now, it should be noted that this type of nonredundancy results in a modification of the predication, adding a boundary or boundaries where none usually are found or softening or removing boundaries where they are normally explicitly present.

2.6. Boundedness and discourse approaches. Where do the discourse grammarians fit into this model we have been developing?

One of the qualities Hopper has associated with the passé simple is sequentiality. In his analysis of a French narrative, he finds that "no event depicted in a passé historique [passé simple] clause overlaps in time with another passé historique sentence" (Hopper 1979b:39).

However, Comrie notes that such is not always the case. Although he considers that "a sequence of forms with perfective meaning will normally be taken to indicate a sequence of events" (Comrie 1976:5), he argues that there are also other possible interpretations. For a sentence such as *the wind tore off the roof, snapped the clothes-line, and brought down the apple-tree,* he offers the following alternative meanings:

> A natural interpretation is to take [the three situations] as events that occurred in succession, each one complete in itself; moreover, they will normally be taken to have occurred in the order in which they are presented in the text. However, this is by no means a necessary interpretation. It is quite possible, even if unlikely, for all three events to have been simultaneous, and this possibility can be made explicit by adding an appropriate adverbial to the sentence: *"the wind simultaneously . . . "* Another possibility is that the speaker is not interested in the relative order of the three events, but is simply registering his observation of the overall result of the wind's damage, in which case he may not even know the actual order of events. (Comrie 1976:5)

It is also possible for one passé simple form to encompass one or two others, as in (12).

(12) *Il fut poli et discret. Sans mot dire, il glissa jusqu'au bout du siège, et tira près de lui son chapeau melon, sur lequel était posée une paire de gants de cuir . . .* (Pagnol 1962:38)

> He **was** [PS] polite and discreet. Without saying a word, he **slid** [PS] to the end of the seat and **pulled** [PS] his bowler hat, on which a pair of leather gloves rested, over next to him.

In this account, the first sentence encompasses the second. The phrase *fut poli et discret* 'was polite and discreet' refers to the action of the second sentence and both sentences thus occupy the same position on a time line.

The other important qualities that discourse grammarians have assigned to the passé simple and the imparfait are, respectively, foregrounding and backgrounding. It has been suggested that this characterization does not hold in every case either. Faucher (1967:364), for example, points out the following unexplained usage in his critique of Weinrich:

> Weinrich refuses to explain this series of imparfaits which the reception speeches at the Académie periodically offer us: "At fifteen, Monsieur, you were carrying off the latin theme award at the Concours General, you were leaving for the Antilles, where you were at last finding a field of exploration as vast as your curiosity, but soon, you were contracting yellow fever, you were being rushed to the hospital and all the doctors were giving

you up..." etc. This parody could be continued for pages and pages. Can one say that these imparfaits make the events they present disappear into the monochrome? It is the reverse which is true... These imparfaits bring the event closer to us, they give it a power of presence that the passé simple would surely take away.

Others have also questioned the concept of foreground tenses and background tenses. Bronzwaer is one who rejects this type of division; he does not believe that the imparfait performs a backgrounding function in discourse. To illustrate his point, he uses the following passage from Murdoch's *The Italian Girl*:

A woman's voice above me softly spoke my name. I paused now and looked up. A face was looking at me over the bannisters, a face which I dimly, partly recognized. Then I realized that it was only my old nurse, the Italian girl. We had had in the house, ever since we were small children, a series of Italian nurserymaids...
(Murdoch 1964:20–21, cited in Bronzwaer 1967:68)

Bronzwaer (1970:68–69) finds that the sentence Weinrich would call backgrounded is actually of greater relative prominence:

The third sentence, containing a progressive form, can only be said to give background information in the sense that the action described here is continuative: the woman had been looking at the I already before he looked at her. The repetitions in this sentence, however, contribute to its dramatic immediacy and thus make it fit the emotionality conveyed by the subjective perspective. Obviously the progressive form does in no way have a "plot-retarding" or "backgrounding" effect.

Thus foregrounding/backgrounding does not appear to be a core characteristic of the passé simple/imparfait opposition. However, the work of Weinrich (1964, 1989), Hopper (1979b), and Thomas (1989) demonstrates that much can be learned about a French narrative text by denoting the passé simple or passé composé as foreground and the imparfait as background. Moreover, discourse analysis approaches based on the foregrounding/backgrounding model have been shown to be effective in the analysis of narrative in a wide variety of languages (Longacre 1968, 1972, 1976, 1981).

What accounts for this discrepancy? It may be that the relationship between the passé simple and foregrounding is one of partial rather than complete correlation. It seems natural that that which is bounded in time can have greater prominence than that which is nonbounded. If the meaning of the passé simple is [+ bounded] and the meaning of the imparfait is [− bounded]; and if a narrative discourse is concerned with Contingent Temporal Succession (after Longacre 1983:3) which requires boundaries; then in a narrative discourse, bounded predicates would tend to compose a foreground, while nonbounded predicates would form a background. These issues are examined more thoroughly in chapter six.

3
Event and State Concepts

Having identified the passé simple with boundedness and the imparfait with nonboundedness, the relationship between these values and the concepts of event and state needs to be determined. Several authors have linked the passé simple with the concept of event. Furthermore, Desclés and Guentchéva have given definitions of event and state which characterize them respectively as a closed (or bounded) interval and an open (or nonbounded) interval.

Other authors, however, appear to define event in terms of subjective rather than objective criteria. The reason for this is found in the nature of communication: it always represents more than one level of abstraction from reality. In a communicational context then, an event is what is perceived or communicated as bounded, and a state is what is perceived or communicated as nonbounded. Thus defined, event and state can be shown to account for a number of abstract or metaphorical uses of the passé simple and the imparfait.

3.1. Definitions. As has been shown, the French grammarians tend to characterize the passé simple in terms of *fait* 'deed, act, action' or *événement* 'event'.

According to Imbs (1960:82), the usage of the passé simple is "closely tied to the notion of event" in such a way that a correct understanding of this notion is necessary in order to use the passé simple correctly. Martin (1971:95) makes a similar statement.

Desclés and Guentchéva take a similar position. They hold that the passé simple always signifies an event while the imparfait, on the other hand, never signifies "an isolated event" (1987:113). It seems, therefore, worthwhile to take some time to understand the concept of event and to define its relation to boundedness and nonboundedness.

In his *Syntax*, Givón (1984:87) distinguishes states, which are "existing conditions not involving change across time" from events, which are "changes across time."

Van Dijk (1977:168–9) also defines event in terms of change, and distinguishes an event from a "state description," which is a "set of propositions" representing a possible world. "Differences between situations are thus represented as differences between state descriptions" (1977:168). As an example of such a difference, van Dijk gives the following two sentences:

(13) *the door is open*
     the door is not open or, *the door is closed*

Since a difference exists between these two descriptions, an event is construed to have occurred between the two situations and time-points that they represent.

Desclés and Guentchéva's (1987:121) definition is similar, stated in terms of change or discontinuity:

> An **event** introduces a discontinuity into a stative situation. Each occurrence of an event is complete in itself without taking into account that which happens before or after.

They define a state as follows:

> A **state** is characterized by a complete absence of change, that is to say, by the absence of any discontinuity; all the phases of the static situation are therefore identical to one another. (p. 118)

A representation of the relationship between event and state which would seem to satisfy all of the above definitions is diagrammed in (14).

(14)   Events and states as objective phenomena

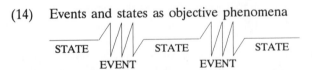

Given the definition of state by Desclés and Guentchéva, it would appear that the transitions between events and states, which would constitute beginnings and endings, would belong to the events rather than the states, as states cannot include any discontinuity. And this turns out to be the case. Desclés and Guentchéva (1987:118) declare that "in a state, there is neither a starting point (which would indicate a change) nor an ending point (which would also indicate a change)."

Desclés and Guentchéva make their definitions clearer with the use of diagrams. They begin with the concept of an interval which they define as "a directed set of contiguous instants ... delimited on the left and on the right by two boundaries that separate the interior (all the instants between the two boundaries) and the exterior (all the instants which are not situated between the two boundaries) of the interval" (1987:117).

Such an interval may be either open or closed, or closed at one end or the other. If the interval is conceived as having a first instant, it is closed on the left; if it has a last instant, it is closed on the right. An interval that has both a first and a last instant is considered to be closed; one that has neither is open.

An interval may also be finite or infinite.[3] If the distance between its two boundaries can be represented by a finite number, then it is finite, if not, it is infinite.

Desclés and Guentchéva represent an event as a closed finite interval. A state would in turn appear as an open interval which may be either finite or infinite but "of which the boundaries are excluded" (p. 118). This would give us the figure [—] for event and ([-)—(-]) or — for state. Thus it appears that event can be represented in the same way as the passé simple, and state in the same way as the imparfait.

3.2. Points of reference: Objective and subjective. In what sense can events be identified with the passé simple and states with the imparfait? The objection will be made that not everything that occurs in the passé simple appears to be an event and, certainly, not everything that appears in the imparfait is a state.

For example, the sentence in (15) appears in the passé simple, but does not represent what we normally would call an event. On the other hand, a sentence such as (16) is not what we would ordinarily understand as a state. Clearly, we need to examine more carefully our definitions of event and state.

(15) *La première quinzaine de juillet fut bien longue.*

The first fifteen days of July were [PS] very long. (Pagnol 1962:63)

---

[3]Desclés and Guentchéva use the terms *borné* and *non-borné*, which would translate as 'bounded' and 'nonbounded,' respectively. To avoid confusion with the concepts of 'open' or 'closed' intervals or with the boundaries that are part of the interval itself, I have taken the liberty of substituting the terms 'finite' and 'infinite' which seem to accurately convey the meaning of Desclés and Guentchéva's terms as they have defined them.

(16) *Pablo criait et pleurait.*

Pablo **was screaming** [IMP] and **crying** [IMP]. (Sartre, cited by
Imbs 1960:91)[4]

Van Dijk and Givón have both defined event in terms of change.
Desclés and Guentchéva have defined it in terms of boundedness as well
as change (or discontinuity).

Imbs is another author who seems to define event in terms of boundedness. Imbs, as we have seen, believes that the concept of event is essential
to the definition of the passé simple. However, his definition of event
contains some elements that are new:

An event is an action that detaches itself from the circumstances
in the midst of which it occurs.

These circumstances can carry it, explain its genesis, or simply
surround or accompany it, but the essential character of an event
is that it detaches itself as a ripe fruit detaches itself from the
tree and continues to exist without it. (1960:82–83)

Imbs (1960:83) also introduces another characteristic into his conception
of event: the effect it has on the observer.

An event produces on its witnesses (audience, hearers, readers,
etc.) an impression of newness, that pushes it, if only for an
instant, to the forefront of current affairs or at least of interest.

Imbs' view of event does permit him to apply it to sentences such as the
following, which would not fit Givón's or Van Dijk's definitions (C. Jullian,
cited by Imbs 1960:84):

(17) *Un des principaux éléments de l'hégémonie de Marseille fut
l'excellence de sa monnaie.*

One of the principal elements of Marseille's hegemony **was** [PS]
the excellence of its currency.

---

[4]For this example, Imbs cites only the name of the author, "Sartre," with no
mention of the specific work in which this sentence appears. This minimal form of
citation seems to be the rule for example sentences given in French grammars. In
these cases, I cannot give a full reference but can only refer the reader to my
intermediate source. Thus, in using such examples in this paper, my practice will be to
give as much of the primary source as I can and then to cite the secondary source in
full: the author's name and year in the text and the full reference in my bibliography.

Weinrich is another who equates the passé simple with the notion of event. He states that the foreground tenses (by which he means the passé simple and passé antérieur) are what cause a story to move and to become "action, intrigue, événement" (1989:130).

He notes that this *événement* that translates motion is often an "unheard of or astonishing event" (*événement inouï*) but concedes that it doesn't necessarily have to be:

> Not every event, however, has to be unheard of in order to seem worthy of being recounted by the speaker and to merit the interest of the hearer. **Nevertheless, it is in the nature of every event worthy of retelling to represent a departure, however feeble, from the uniformity and normality of the flat, monot-onous "everyday."** (1989:130)

It would seem that both Imbs and Weinrich set more stringent defini-tions of event than the other authors. To the simple definition of 'change', they would add the stipulation that it must be somehow out-of-the-ordinary, unexpected.

These two different conceptions of an event would seem to correspond to the following definitions given in Webster's Dictionary (1975:396).

(18)   event   1a: something that happens: OCCURRENCE
              1b: a noteworthy happening.

While the first definition seems to be quite objective, the second neces-sarily involves subjective elements, there being no way to scientifically determine noteworthiness. Which of these two concepts comes closest to defining the use of the passé simple?

Imbs and Weinrich both clearly link the passé simple with a subjective concept of event, that is, one involving a subjective view of what is noteworthy.

Comrie (1976:51) defines an event as "a dynamic situation viewed per-fectively." He thus seems to equate the passé simple with a particular way of viewing what is objectively an event, e.g., with a subjective view of an event. His definition of an event thus contains both objective and subjec-tive elements.

I propose that we posit these two concepts of event: (1) an event as measured empirically, in terms of change or discontinuity, and (2) an event as perceived by a given individual on the basis of subjective criteria. These criteria may or may not include the notion of 'noteworthiness'.

3.3–3.5 Levels of abstraction

On what basis can we distinguish two such concepts of event? To answer this question, let us turn our attention to a different set of distinctions—those between phenomena, perception, and communication. These distinctions are only what we would expect. All communication is removed from the empirical, and a proper conceptualization of this relationship actually requires three levels (one objective and two subjective) rather than two. These levels can be represented as in (19).

(19)   Levels of abstraction in communication

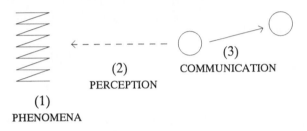

3.3. Level one: Phenomena. At the lowest level, we have the situation itself. 'Situation' here means the objective reality, and it may be a state, a process, or an event.

3.4. Level two: Perception. This situation may be perceived by an observer or an audience, and this perception constitutes a second level. As we have seen earlier, Grobe (1967:344–45) has described this level in terms of a list of possible scenarios. They are as follows:

1. The observer can see the entire action from beginning to end.
2. He is aware only of the beginning boundary or only of the ending boundary of the action.
3. The action has such short duration that it appears to the observer to have only one single time boundary.
4. The observer arrives on the scene after the beginning or before the end of the action or state. In this way, he does not see the temporal boundary (or boundaries) in question and thus does not have a real awareness of it (or them).
5. An action has such a long duration that its beginning and end are "beyond the horizon of [an observer's] temporal imagination."

6. An action with definite boundaries "possesses such an absorbing dynamic character that [the observer becomes] more interested in it as pure movement, abstracted from all chronology."

The other element of Desclés and Guentchéva's definition of an event is that it is dynamic as opposed to static. This is an opposition that is found in Comrie, as well. The dynamic/static opposition is something that is subject to different perceptions by different individuals. Comrie (1976:35) points this out in regard to perception type verbs:

> The relevant factor seems to be that it is possible to view raining, seeing, hearing, etc., either as states or as non-states (dynamic situations): different psychological theories differ as to just how active a process perception is, and there is no reason to suppose that language presupposes the answer by uniquely classifying perception as either a state or a dynamic situation.

3.5. Level three: Communication. The third level is that of communication. The observer communicates his perception of what occurred to someone else. At this level also, changes may occur in the information. Dahl recognizes this fact, namely that "one and the same (individual) situation may be described in different ways." He thus calls for a taxonomy of "descriptions or characterizations of situations" rather than a taxonomy of situations (1985:27–28). He gives examples of a single situation described by two different sentences:

> Seeing John sitting at his desk, we may answer the question **What is he doing?** by using either ... **He is writing** [or] ... **He is writing a letter** ... Both these sentences can thus be said to describe the same situation. (1981:83)

This kind of variation in the way that a situation is described amounts to a choice that constitutes the freedom of the author. He can choose to leave out information or to include it. As a matter of fact, the limitations imposed on him by his genre force him to make these kinds of decisions. Also, a skillful author recognizes that he has choices, not only in what information to leave out or to present but in how he perceives and structures his information.

Several discourse grammarians have recognized this freedom of the author and the limitation it imposes on their ability to give a complete characterization of the passé simple or imparfait in terms of verb correlations.

Halliday, for example, sees a discourse as organized into a linear succession of "information units." The author "is free to decide where each information unit begins and ends, and how it is structured internally"

(1967:200). And he is free as well to decide which of these units are to be focussed (p. 204).

Thomas (1989:35–6), in his study of prominence, states that the "whole idea of prominence . . . originates from [the author's] *freedom* to decide which element in an information unit should be stressed."

As we have seen, Weinrich gives a list of verbs that he finds to occur most often in the passé simple and of verbs that occur most often in the imparfait. He is careful to add that "the decision to underline or not to underline, to highlight or not to highlight a certain verb for the hearer, by placing this verb in a foreground tense, belongs basically to each narrator" (Weinrich 1989:133).

To define the passé simple as 'event' and the imparfait as 'state' in a subjective sense of these terms recognizes the narrator's freedom to differ, sometimes quite significantly, from what might be considered an objective definition of these concepts.

The resultant degree of skewing that occurs between levels of phenomena and communication[5] is sometimes such that the terms 'event' and 'state' become metaphorical in their meaning.

3.6. Event and state as metaphor. What kinds of examples might show the use of the passé simple to depict a metaphorical event or the use of the imparfait to depict a metaphorical state? The passage from *Un coeur simple* was given earlier as an example of Reid's focus theory. We consider it again to see if it supports only such a theory as his:

(20) *Pendant un demi-siècle les bourgeoises de Pont-l'Evêque envièrent à Mme. Aubain sa servante Félicité.*

Pour cent francs par an, elle faisait la cuisine et le ménage, cousait, lavait, repassait, savait brider un cheval, engraisser les volailles, battre le beurre, et resta fidèle à sa maîtresse,—qui cependant n'était pas une personne agréable. (Flaubert 1965:150)

For half a century the middle class women of Pont-l'Evêque envied Mme. Aubain her servant Félicité.

For one hundred francs a year, she **did** the cooking and the housecleaning, **sewed, washed, ironed, knew** how to bridle a horse, fatten chickens, churn butter and **remained** faithful to her mistress,—who was not, however, easy to get along with.

---

[5]There is a fourth level, that of the hearer/reader, but we do not have occasion to discuss it here.

Reid saw the first five verbs as representing "weak concentration of focus" and the final one as representing "strong concentration of focus." On examining these verbs, we notice that the only one that is in the passé simple is what we would usually refer to as a stative verb, *resta* 'stayed or remained'.

Obviously, this predicate, which is one of low dynamism and little change, cannot represent a real world event; however, the theme of this story seems to show that the author is regarding his character's faithfulness and simplicity of heart as out-of-the-ordinary and worthy of retelling. Thus it seems that 'remaining faithful' can be regarded as an event in the subjective sense that we have already established.

The use of the passé simple adds an element of boundaries to the verb *rester*, resulting in a sense of globality that can be expressed as "in everything she did, all her activities, she remained faithful."

What of the verbs (in boldface) in the imparfait that seem, for the most part, to be dynamic actions? Can these be considered to represent states?

In order to answer that question, it is necessary to take into account the sense of these verbs when they are put into this context in the imparfait. The markers *pendant un demi-siècle* 'for half a century' and *par an* 'by year' set a time frame that gives these actions the sense of repetition and habituality. As we will see in chapter five, habitual actions can be seen as states or states of affairs.

Thus it appears that the verb usage in this passage can be considered as event and state in a metaphorical sense.

Another use of the passé simple that seems difficult to explain is Imbs' example of an event, also given earlier in this chapter (C. Jullian, cited by Imbs 1960:84).

(21) *Un des principaux éléments de l'hégémonie de Marseille **fut** l'excellence de sa monnaie.*

One of the principal elements of Marseille's hegemony **was** [PS] the excellence of its currency.

As in Reid's passage above, the verb in this sentence, *être*, is not one which is usually used to encode an event. However, the passé simple here gives it a boundedness that causes it to stand out in relation to other stative verbs that might be used in the text. Thus the passé simple is used here, it seems, in its secondary sense of 'foregrounding'. It can be considered to mean 'event' only in a metaphorical sense.

4
Event and State in Relation to Verb Types

Before looking at the range of uses of the passé simple and imparfait, we look at the inherent qualities of different verbs. What natural categories do verbs fall into? Can they be categorized in terms of their use in event or state predications? What is the relationship between verbal categories and the imparfait/passé simple distinction?

4.1. Vendler's four verb types. The groundwork for verb classification was done by philosophers. In 1957, Zeno Vendler published a short article in the *Philosophical Review,* entitled "Verbs and Times," in which he presented a four-way division of verbs. His method was to distinguish verb classes in terms of the questions that could be posed or could not be posed about specific verbs.

For example, he found that he could distinguish verbs that have a continuous tense in English from those that do not on the basis of the question, "What are you doing?" He found that the group with continuous tenses (including such verbs as *run, write,* and *work*) answered this question but that the other group did not. On the other hand, he found that the group lacking continuous tenses (and including such verbs as *know, love,* and *recognize*) answered the question "Do you [verb]?," while the other group did not (1967:99).

Vendler next examined verbs that can be used in the continuous (*be + -ing*) tense and made a division within this category. He noted that there is a difference between such continuous situations as *running* and *drawing a circle* in that if someone starts running and stops in the next moment, it is nevertheless true that he has run. If, however, someone has just started drawing a circle and then stops, it may not be true that he has drawn a circle. Vendler defines this difference in terms of the verb having or not having a terminal point which must be reached. He shows that for verbs which have a terminal point the appropriate question is "How long did it **take** to do x?," whereas for verbs that do not have terminal points, the appropriate question is "**For** how long did he do x?" (p. 100–01). Vendler calls the verbs that do not have a terminal point ACTIVITIES and those that do ACCOMPLISHMENTS.

Finally he examines the categories of verbs that cannot be used in the continuous tense. These break down into two more distinct categories: those that admit the question "At what time did x happen?" (such as *reach* in *reach the top* and *spot* in *spot the plane*) and those that admit the question "For how long did x last?" (such as *love* and *believe in the stork*) (p. 102). The first category he names ACHIEVEMENT TERMS and the second STATE TERMS.

Vendler's system thus contains four verb types: STATES, ACTIVITIES, ACCOMPLISHMENTS, and ACHIEVEMENTS.[6]

Vendler (1967:113–14) also noted that, curiously, some verbs could fall into more than one category. He gives the example of *smoke* which he categorizes as an activity in *are you smoking?* and as a state in *do you smoke?* He also mentions *see*, which he classifies as a state in such common usages as *I see it* but which can also act as an achievement in *at that moment, I saw him.*

4.2. Kenny's three verb types. Working independently, Kenny (1963) came up with a similar breakdown of verb types. He too takes the continuous tense distinction as his point of departure. However, he sees the verbs which do not take continuous tenses as forming only one class, that of STATES. The verbs which do take continuous tenses he divides into two classes: ACTIVITIES and PERFORMANCES. He makes this distinction on the basis of the propositions that are true about these groups of verbs. If "A is 0ing" implies that "A has 0ed," then the verb falls into the category of activity. If "A is 0ing" implies that "A has not 0ed," then the verb is classified as a performance (1963:172–3).

As for states, Kenny notes that the proposition "A has 0ed" implies that "A 0s" (p. 173). He also distinguishes the three categories in terms of type of duration: a state "lasts for" a time, an activity "goes on for a time," and a performance "takes" time (p. 176).

Kenny (1963:175) gives the following examples of his verb categories:

---

[6]Other methods of categorizing verbs have also been used. Notably, Wallace Chafe (1970) classified verbs according to the case roles of the nouns they required. His categories were: States (N=Patient); Processes (N=patient); Activities or Actions (N=Agent); Process-Actions (N1=Agent; N2=Patient); and Ambient verbs (V=State or V=Action).

(22)   Static   Performance   Activity

      understand   discover   listen to
      know how   learn   keep (a secret)
      love   find   weep
      mean   kill   laugh
      fear   convince   talk
      be blue   grow up   live (at Rome)
              build (a house)
              wash

4.3. Garey: Telic versus atelic verb types. While the philosophers were attempting to describe categories of verbs, linguists were working on some of the same problems from a different angle, that of aspect. In the same year as Vendler's original article, Garey published a paper on French verbal aspect in which he recognized that imperfective forms of verbs sometimes differed in the relation that they bore to their perfective counterparts. Using an example given by Sten (1952:25), he claimed that, while *il se noyait* 'he was drowning' did not necessarily imply *il s'est noyé* 'he drowned' in the opinion of most French speakers, *ils jouaient au bridge* 'they were playing bridge' did imply *ils ont joué au bridge* 'they played bridge' (Garey 1957:104–5).

Garey gave the term TELIC to constructions such as *il se noyait* (Vendler's ACCOMPLISHMENT) and the term ATELIC to those such as *ils jouaient au bridge* (Vendler's ACTIVITY).

The discovery of this distinction led Garey (1957:109) to distinguish between LEXICAL ASPECT and GRAMMATICAL ASPECT and to posit the following set of interactions between the two:

(1) A perfective construction implies an imperfective. If it is true perfectively, it is true imperfectively; e.g. *il s'est noyé* implies *il se noyait*—'he drowned' implies 'he was drowning' . . .

(2) An atelic construction in an imperfective tense implies a corresponding construction in a perfective tense; e.g., *il nageait* implies *il a nagé*.

(3) Telic imperfective does not imply telic perfective; e.g., *il se noyait* does not imply *il s'est noyé*.

4.4. Comrie's situation types. Building on Vendler (1957) and Garey (1957), Comrie (1976) made binary distinctions between a state and a dynamic situation, between a durative and a punctual situation, and between a telic and an atelic situation. A suggested diagram of his scheme and its relation to Vendler's verb types is given in (23).

(23)   Comrie: Distinctions between situation types

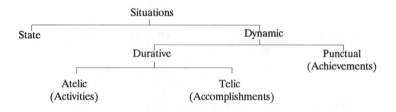

Comrie relates these to the traditional terms of state, process, and event through the interworking of situation type and grammatical aspect, as diagrammed in (24).

(24)   Comrie: Interaction of aspect and situation types

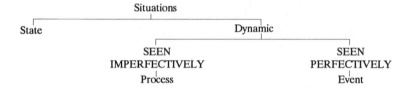

Combining these two diagrams would give us the following chart showing how these verb types are affected by a change of aspect:

(25)   Aspect and situation categories

	Static	Atelic	Telic	Punctual
IMP	state	process	process	—
PS	?[7]	event	event	event

Since we have been equating the term atelic with nonboundedness and the term telic with boundedness, this chart might be seen as a refinement of an earlier chart (see (11) in §2.5), with static and atelic verbs combined

---

[7]Comrie does not categorize this type of passé simple. However, we will consider it in §5.3.

into the category of [−bounded] and telic verbs combined into the category of [+bounded]. However, this system breaks down, and we will see why in the next section.

4.5. Mourelatos' situation categories. Mourelatos (1978:415) gives two main criticisms of the Vendler-Kenny verb scheme: (1) it does not take verbal aspect into account, and (2) its classifications are too narrow, amounting to a "specification in the context of human agency of the more fundamental, topic-neutral trichotomy, event-process-state."

As evidence of his first criticism, Mourelatos shows how Vendler's cases of 'achievement' uses of 'stative' verbs can be accounted for by the concept of perfective versus imperfective aspect (p. 419). For example, *see* with imperfective aspect (*I am seeing* or *I was seeing*) would correspond to Vendler's category of 'state', while *see* in the perfective (*at that moment, I saw* . . .) would correspond to his category of 'achievement'.

Mourelatos next argues that the perfomance-activity-state verb scheme is only a more specific form of the old event-process-state trichotomy. The distinction is that event-process-state is a topic neutral breakdown, whereas performance-activity-state contains the concept of human agency. He develops his own scheme (1978:423) shown in (26).

(26)   Mourelatos' situation types[8]

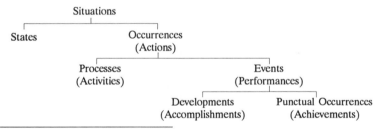

---

[8]Mourelatos divides predications into two basic categories corresponding to the count and mass categories of nouns. Event predications carry the feature COUNT in such a way that a sentence such as *Vesuvius erupted three times* could be described by a corresponding nominalization, *there were three eruptions of Vesuvius*, or a sentence such as *Mary capsized the boat* could be described by the nominalization, *there was a capsizing of the boat by Mary* (1978:425). Nonevent (process and state) predications, on the other hand, carry the feature MASS and cannot be quantified by a cardinal count adverbial. For example, *Jones was painting the nativity* could only be described by a nonquantified transcription such as *there was painting of the nativity by Jones* (pp. 426–27). This count versus mass distinction, which opposes events to processes and states, nicely supports the bounded/nonbounded distinction we have made. Obviously, only that which is bounded can be quantified.

Mourelatos points out another problem with Vendler's and Kenny's work: their focus is on verbs rather than predications (a concern that Comrie (1976:45) also mentions). He points out that most linguists prefer to speak of predicate rather than verb types.

As a demonstration of the problems of classifying verbs, he shows that one verb can be found in all four types of predication, e.g., the verb *hear* in (27) (Mourelatos 1978:423–24).

(27) State: *I hear you well.*
      Process: *I'm hearing buzzing sounds.*
      Development: *I heard him sing a serenade.*
      Punctual occurrence: *I heard him cough.*

Mourelatos claims that Vendler's typology, when broadened in the ways that he indicates, can account for predications that have no agent. He illustrates this (p. 423) with the examples in (28).

(28) State: *The air smells of jasmine.*
      Process: *It's snowing.*
      Development: *The sun went down.*
      Punctual occurrence: *The cable snapped.*

4.6. Mourelatos' aspectual distinctions applied to French. Mourelatos' examples are mostly in English, a language that does not have a grammatical perfective-imperfective opposition as such. It is thus easier to see his distinctions when examples are taken from French.

For example, to exhibit a perfective-imperfective difference, Mourelatos is, in some cases, forced to oppose the past tense to the present, due to the fact that a state in English (as mentioned previously) cannot take the past progressive. This can be seen in (29) by comparing a few of his examples given above.

(29) State: *I hear you well.*
                            The air smells of jasmine.
      Development: *I heard him sing a serenade.*
                            The sun went down.

Since the present tense has no perfective form, Mourelatos' development examples must be in the past tense, and, since a state cannot take the past progressive (the only English past imperfective form), his state examples must either be in the present or in the past perfective.

These distinctions are thus less clearcut than could be desired in English. When these situations are put into the past tense and translated into French, a very clear line appears, in the past tense, to separate state-process from development-punctual occurrence.

The verb *see*, mentioned by Vendler, for example, must be a state in the imperfective: *je vois/je voyais* [PRES/IMP] and an achievement in the perfective: *je vis* [PS].

Mourelatos' examples of his four types demonstrate in (30) the same purely aspectual break.

(30)	State:	*Je vous entendais* [IMP] *bien.*
		L'air sentait [IMP] *le jasmin.*
	Process:	*J'entendais* [IMP] *des sons bourdonnants.*
		Il neigeait [IMP]*.*
	Development:	*Je l'entendis* [PS] *chanter une sérénade.*
		Le soleil se coucha [PS]*.*
	Punctual occurrence:	*Je l'entendis tousser* [PS]*.*
		Le cable se brisa [PS]*.*

As Mourelatos showed in English, a change from imperfective to perfective aspect can transform a state into a punctual occurrence. If, for example, *je vous entendais bien*, is changed to *je vous entendis bien*, the meaning of the verb becomes 'I understood you well', as in 'I grasped what you said'.

Perfective aspect can thus be seen to correlate, at least in the main, with event propositions (development and punctual occurrence), and imperfective aspect with state propositions. Furthermore, as can be seen in these examples, the perfectivity or imperfectivity of the verb often seems to determine the predicate type, a perfective form tending to produce either a development or a punctual occurrence, and an imperfective form tending to produce either a state or an activity.

Mourelatos has discovered that there is yet another kind of verb—one that is not strongly [+bounded] or [−bounded] but is more or less neutral in this regard. His term for this quality is SEMANTIC MULTIVALENCE (1981:196). If such a verb is used in the passé simple, it becomes [+bounded]. If it is used in the imparfait, it becomes [−bounded]. We can thus see three types of verbs or predicates that could be placed in a chart as in (31).

(31) Combination of bounded and nonbounded types with Mourelatos' multivalent type

Predication Types

Tense-aspect	[−bounded]	[+bounded]	[neutral]
Imparfait [−bounded]	−(−bounded)	−(+bounded)	−(bounded)
Passé simple [+bounded]	+(−bounded)	+(+bounded)	+(bounded)

The two predication types, [−bounded] and [+bounded], would correspond roughly to Garey's atelic and telic categories. The combinations −(−bounded) and +(+bounded) would correspond to marked predicate types used with an identically marked aspect. The mixed combinations, +(−bounded) and −(+bounded) would correspond to Abrate's emphasis categories (see example (1) in chapter one). In these cases, the boundedness value of the aspect (+ or −) would override the inherent value of the predicate. The third verb category, the one that seems to be unmarked or very weakly marked for boundedness, would correspond to Mourelatos' findings and would have different senses or meanings according to the aspect used.

It would probably be most correct to speak not of verb categories in relation to boundedness but rather of a continuum of boundedness, with different verbs occupying various places along the line. Such a continuum might be conceptualized as in (32).

(32) |———————————————|
      + bounded   neutral   − bounded

5
Event and State in Different Uses of the Imparfait and Passé Simple

Short definitions of the imparfait and the passé simple often are given, though many grammarians find it necessary to give extensive examples of particular uses of the imparfait in specific contexts. They do this to cover the full range of particular uses in a way that their short definitions do not. With the exception of Imbs, they do not give any unifying principle that underlies all of the particular uses. Imbs (1960:90) suggests such a principle, but does not emphasize it in his work. In this chapter, such a principle is emphasized as the specific uses of the imparfait are examined.

5.1. Categories of examples. Grammarians tend to devote more space to the uses of the imparfait than to the uses of the passé simple. The *Grammaire Larousse* (1964) does not categorize examples of the passé simple but gives three categories of usage for the imparfait: temporal, indirect style, and modal.

Imbs (1960) also devotes more attention to the imparfait. Although he gives only a definition and a few examples of the passé simple, he lists eight pages of distinct uses, with examples, of the imparfait. These include an imparfait of anterior circumstances, opening, simultaneous or posterior actions, commentary or reflection, a 'classical' imparfait-passé simple opposition, an imparfait of attempt, an imparfait of picturesque, of rupture or closing, consequence, indirect style, free indirect style, habit, and progression. In addition, Imbs gives modal and stylistic uses of the imparfait.

Grévisse (1980:834) also gives a long list of uses of the imparfait that various authors have distinguished including an imparfait of habit or repetition, of duration, of false simultaneity, of description, of progression, of explanation, of free indirect style, of cause, and of attempt.

Grévisse, however, rejects this compartmentalization of usage and maintains that in all of these examples, the imparfait "has no other temporal value than its specific value which is to indicate the unfolding of a process in duration" (p. 835).[9] In Grévisse's view, the examples above are not distinct uses or values of the imparfait but are all explainable in terms of one temporal value of the imparfait which he defines in terms of duration. His approach is correct in that he assumes a single form has a unifying definition. But, as in chapter three, the concept of duration does not provide a definition which is general enough to explain the full range of examples which we find.

The purpose of this section is to demonstrate that all of the uses of the imparfait can be explained in terms of the author's viewing the situation as a state or as having one or more of the qualities associated with a state. State is used in the sense of either (1) an existing condition not involving change across time (Givón 1984:87), or (2) a set of circumstances, etc. characterizing a person or thing; condition (Webster's 1971:419).

The distinction between these two definitions can perhaps be shown by calling the first, state, and the second, state of affairs. Both of these definitions share the quality of nonboundedness discussed previously. In order to illustrate the nature of the imparfait when it occurs in opposition to the passé simple, the following symbolization is used in many of the examples. An event (recounted in the passé simple) will be represented by a point (●) because the boundaries are focal and the internal structure is not. A state (depicted in the imparfait) will be represented by a horizontal line (—) because the internal structure is focal and the boundaries are not.

5.2–5.11 Imparfait: Uses

5.2. Circumstance or description. Imbs characterizes this usage of the imparfait as "anterior circumstance" to a passé simple form. The example he gives is in (33) (Alphonse Daudet, cited by Imbs 1960:90). In fact, the usage in this example is for a state which is anterior, simultaneous, and posterior to the event given in the passé simple. This is clearly an example of state as background to an event.

(33) *Numa Roumestan avait vingt ans quand il vint terminer à Paris son droit, commencé à Aix.*

---

[9]Grévisse does list several uses of the imparfait that he considers to be special cases. Except for the narrative or picturesque imparfait, these seem to be uses that are classed as modal or stylistic by Imbs.

Numa Roumestan was twenty years old [IMP] when he came [PS] to Paris to complete his [studies in] law, begun in Aix.

Lasserre and Grandjean (1948:105) term this use the *imparfait simultané*. Their example is in (34).

(34) *Il pleuvait à torrents pendant le passage du cortège*

It was pouring down rain [IMP] during the passing of the procession.

The authors are emphasizing the simultaneous nature of the two situations. We can see that the imparfait is describing a nonbounded state over which the event is superimposed.

According to Lasserre and Grandjean, the *imparfait simultané* becomes the *imparfait descriptif* when it describes the things that surround the action proper (p. 105). For an example, they give the following passage in which all of the main clause verbs are imparfait forms.

(35) *La grande houle, presque éternelle dans ses régions, était molle et s'en allait comme en mourant. C'étaient de longues montagnes d'eau aux formes douces et arrondies... Elles passaient et il en venait toujours.* (P. Loti, cited in Lasserre and Grandjean 1948:105)

The great wave, of almost eternal spread, **was** soft and **moved** as if dying. It **was** [composed of] long mountains of water soft and round in shape... These **moved on** and **were** continually **succeeded** by new ones.

This example does not give an event, but it does present a nonbounded state and seems to be setting the stage for an upcoming event.

Grévisse (1980:834) also gives, as one of his so-called values of the imparfait, an "imparfait de description," which is considered as painting the circumstances, the setting in which a situation occurs, the material or psychological aspect of a being. As an example he gives the following (Hugo, Chât., 13, 1; cited by Grévisse 1969:105):

(36) *Il neigeait. On etait vaincu par sa conquête./ Pour la premiere fois l'aigle baissait la tête.*

It **was snowing** [IMP]. They **were** [IMP] vanquished by the conquest./ For the first time, the eagle **was hanging** [IMP] his head.

Again, no event is given but it can be assumed that the stage is being set for an event. Clearly, no boundaries are in focus in this example.

Using the symbolization that I defined earlier we can see that the examples in (33) and (34) can be represented by —•—. The situation in the imparfait is anterior, simultaneous, and posterior to the situation in the passé simple. The examples in (35) and (36) can be represented by — where we are expecting an event to eventually be placed on this continuum.

5.3. Imparfait-passé simple: Classical opposition. Imbs describes the classical opposition use of the imparfait with the passé simple as a state-event opposition. In his words:

> The classical opposition is that which evokes in a first proposition the state which was in effect in the past (imparfait) and in a second the event (in the passé simple) which occurred to interrupt or to change the indefinite course of the process evoked by the imparfait. (Imbs 1960:91)

An example of this usage is seen in (37) (Flaubert 1972:21, cited by Imbs 1960:91).

(37) *Nous **étions** à l'étude, quand le Proviseur **entra**, suivi d'un nouveau habillé en bourgeois et d'un garçon de classe qui portait un grand pupitre.*

We **were** [IMP] at our schoolwork, when the principal **entered** [PS], followed by a well-dressed new student and another student who was carrying a large desk.

This kind of imparfait-passé simple opposition shows an anterior state disturbed by an event, which can be represented as —•.

This same configuration applies to another use described by both Imbs and Grévisse: that of the imparfait of attempt (*de tentative*). This opposition occurs when a first situation in progress or at its beginning is interrupted by a second action or situation. An example of this is given by Grévisse in (38) (Vigny, Poèmes mod., *La Prison*, cited by le Bidois, cited by Grévisse 1980:834).

(38) *Les pleurs qu'il **retenait** coulèrent un moment.*

The tears that he was **holding back** [IMP] flowed [PS] for a moment.

Imbs (1960:92) gives a more elliptical example which uses an implied passé simple or passé composé as well as a present in (39). The event (implied) occurred when the listener found the speaker; the state of affairs was that he was going out.

(39) *Vous avez de la chance [de me rencontrer]: je sortais . . .*

You're lucky [PRES] [to find me here]: I was going out [IMP].

Even though 'going out' is unquestionably an action, unlike 'being at' one's schoolwork or 'holding back tears', it can be seen that the configuration for this example is ——•, the same as for the other examples in this section. All are examples of an ongoing situation that was affected by a second, intervening situation. We again see that the unifying principle applies: Each use of the imparfait corresponds to a nonbounded state. In each of the cases above, a boundary is introduced by the passé simple.

5.4. Duration. Examples of the imparfait of duration are given by Grévisse and also by Lasserre and Grandjean (1948:105). The example given by Lasserre and Grandjean, and categorized as indeterminate duration (*durée indéterminée*), is *les Egyptiens croyaient à la métempsychose* 'the Egyptians believed [IMP] in reincarnation'. Clearly this involves a cognitive **state.**

A similar example is given by Grévisse in (40) (Montesq., Consid. 10, cited by Grévisse 1980:834).

(40) *Les citoyens romains **regardaient** le commerce et les arts comme des occupations d'esclaves: ils ne les **exerçaient** point.*

Roman citizens **regarded** [IMP] commerce and the arts as slave occupations: they did not **exercise** [IMP] them.

It is difficult to see in what way these examples of the imparfait differ from those given above. Can these situations not be considered circumstance or descriptions of a people or a period of time? The factor which distinguishes these examples from those in §5.3 is that they do not necessarily provide a setting for an event.

The representation for these situations would thus be ——, indicating a state with no particular event involved.

5.5. Background. Imbs lists the background (*fond de décor*) use, describing it as common among modern authors who "like to present, as an afterthought, simultaneous or posterior actions as background to the main action" (1960:90). He gives the example in (41) (Victor Hugo, cited by Imbs 1960:90).

(41) *Le soir vint, les théâtres n'ouvrirent pas; les patrouilles circulaient d'un air irrité, on fouillait les passants; on arrêtait les suspects.*

Evening came [PS], the theaters did not open [PS]; patrols **circulated** [IMP] with an air of irritation, passersby **were searched** [IMP]; suspects **were arrested** [IMP].

The **coup** that Imbs refers to is a time boundary and perhaps an unrealized event. The imparfait clauses are presenting simultaneous or posterior actions which are presented as a state of affairs as there are no boundaries in focus. Imbs shows the same pattern in (42) (Sartre, cited by Imbs 1960:91).

(42) *Le garagiste la rattrappa au vol et la remit sur pied. Pablo criait et pleurait.*

The garage man caught [PS] it again in mid-flight and put [PS] it back on its feet. Pablo was screaming [IMP] and crying [IMP].

Despite the fact that the verbs used in the imparfait in these examples are dynamic, they form the background or set of circumstances against which the action occurred. Thus this opposition of the imparfait and passé simple has the same representation as the examples in §5.2: —●—.

Imbs also notes that, within a sentence, a subordinate clause beginning with a temporal *comme* 'as, while' almost requires an imperfective main verb. He gives the example in (43) (Simenon, cited by Imbs 1960:91).

(43) *On l'a tuée? demanda-t-elle, comme Maigret s'asseyait près de la fenêtre.*

"Has she been killed?," she asked [PS], **as** Maigret **sat down** [IMP] near the window.

Comme in this sense seems able to put almost any verb in the imparfait—any verb, that is, which can form part of a predicate with durative meaning. The length of duration here is not important, but the situation must be one that can have some duration, i.e., a nonpunctual situation. Only a durative situation can be seen as a state or a state of affairs against which an event occurred.

Weinrich (1989:133) gives a list of verbs which he believes will most naturally take the passé simple, since they "signify an event."

(44) *dire*   say   *recevoir* receive   *répondre*   respond
      arrêter   stop   *prendre* take   *entendre*   hear
      reprendre take back   *poser*   put down   *mettre*   put
      partir   leave   *ouvrir*   open   *ajouter*   add
      revenir   return   *entrer*   enter   *reconnaître* recognize
      obtenir   obtain

Most of these, however, can follow *comme* as imparfait forms as in (45).

(45) a. *Comme il disait cela, il leva son stylo.*
         As he **was saying** [IMP] that, he lifted [PS] his pen.
      b. *Comme il prenait le livre, il me remercia.*
         As he **was taking** [IMP] the book, he thanked [PS] me.
      c. *Comme il mettait son manteau, il dit ...*
         As he **was putting on** [IMP] his coat, he said [PS] ...
      d. *Comme il arrêtait la voiture, il vit ...*
         As he **was stopping** [IMP] his car, he saw [PS] ...
      e. *Comme il posait son stylo, il me donna un clin d'oeil.*
         As he **was putting down** [IMP] his pen, he winked [PS].

These are another example of ——●——, since the passé simple predicate
seems to be conceived as occurring during the imparfait action. The
imparfait action becomes the backdrop for, or state which obtained during,
the passé simple action.

5.6. Commentary. Another use of the imparfait noted by Imbs and the
Grammaire Larousse is to present commentary or reflections on the actions occurring in the passé simple.

Imbs (1960:91) would put in this category also "the analysis of a docu-
ment, of an observation, of an intention." He gives the example in (46)
(Voltaire, Histoire de Charles XII, Livre VIII, cited by Imbs 1960:91).

(46) *Voici les conditions préliminaires de cette alliance, qui **devait**
     changer la face de l'Europe, telles qu'elles furent trouvées dans les
     papiers de Görtz, après sa mort. Le czar, retenant pour lui la
     Livonie, et une partie de l'Ingrie et de Carélie, **rendait** à la Suède
     tout le reste; il **s'unissait** avec Charles XII dans le dessein de
     rétablir le roi Stanislas sur le trône de Pologne, et **s'engageait** à
     rentrer dans ce pays avec quatre-vingt mille Moscovites pour
     détrôner ce même roi Auguste, en faveur duquel il avait fait dix
     ans la guerre.*

Here are the conditions that predated this alliance, which **was going** [IMP] to change the face of Europe, such as they were found in the papers of Görtz, after his death. The czar, retaining for himself Livonia and a part of Ingria and of Carelia, **was giving** [IMP] everything else back to Sweden; he **was uniting** [IMP] with Charles XII in the design of reestablishing King Stanislas on the Polish throne, and **was committing** himself [IMP] to reenter this country with eighty thousand Muscovites in order to dethrone King Augustus, the same king in favor of whom he had made war for ten years.

In this passage, it can be seen that the alliance is the event and that what is being presented is its background or backdrop: the political situation currently obtaining in Europe. Thus, although the situations described are actions in progress, *le czar rendait à la Suède tout le reste,* they are seen as representing a state or state of affairs, which, as the author points out, was going to be changed as a result of the event, i.e., the new alliance. The configuration would thus be —● (or —●—).

Other examples that Imbs gives of commentary on an event are in (47) and (48) (Sartre; Simenon cited by Imbs 1960:91).

(47) *Elle courut à l'auto, elle voulait la réveiller tout de suite.*

She ran [PS] to the car, she **wanted** [IMP] to wake her up immediately.

(48) *Il dut détourner la tête, car il était sur le point de pleurer.*

He had [PS] to turn his head away, because he **was** [IMP] on the verge of tears.

In these the event is explained in terms of a state of emotions which motivated it. The configuration would therefore be —●—, since the emotional state probably continued for a period of time after the event.

The *Grammaire Larousse* gives an example which can be clearly seen to be event and state-as-background or description in (49) (Aragon, cited by the *Grammaire Larousse* 1964:347) and another which appears rather to be event and state-as-consequence (or result) in (50) (Rais, cited by the *Grammaire Larousse* 1964:347).

(49) *La porte s'ouvrit et Ph. François Touchard entra, qui* vint *faire ses dévotions à ses dames. C'était encore un bel homme.*

The door **opened** [PS] and Ph. François Touchard **entered** [PS], who **came** [PS] to pay his respects to his ladies. He **was** [IMP] still a handsome man.

(50) *Eliane occupa bientôt mon esprit. Ma solitude prenait fin.*

Eliane soon **occupied** [PS] my mind. My solitude **was coming** [IMP] to an end.

Grévisse, in his list of values of the imparfait (values, that is, which others have listed but which he himself does not recognize), gives an example of an imparfait of explanation which also seems to fit into the commentary category shown in (51) (Voltaire, *Micromégas*, III, cited by Le Bidois, cited also by Grévisse 1980:834).

(51) *Enfin ils aperçurent une petite lueur, c'était la terre.*

Finally, they caught sight of [PS] a small glimmer of light, it **was** [IMP] the earth.

In all of these cases, the configuration would be ——●——, representing a state which is anterior, simultaneous, and posterior to the previously mentioned event.

5.7. Perspective or indirect style. Imbs also gives an imparfait of 'indirect style', which, in his view, "marks that the subordinated action, even if present, is seen in the psychological prolongation of the principal action situated in the past" (Imbs 1960:94).

The characteristic of this style seems to be that it occurs in a subordinate clause following a main clause which contains a verb of speech or thought. Its use appears to derive from the character of such a situation as a cognitive or psychological state. It is as if the thoughts or words of a character were paraphrased (Sartre; F. Mauriac cited by Imbs 1960:94):

(52) *Je croyais que c'était mon nègre.*

I **thought** [IMP] that he **was** [IMP] my negro.

(53) *Tout à coup là, je viens de comprendre que vous étiez à la hauteur de ce sacrifice.*

Suddenly there, I've just understood [PRES] that you **were** [IMP] capable of that sacrifice.

We can see that this first example represents two states: one cognitive and the other equative, both of which are clearly nonbounded. The second shows an event in the present and a state in the past. The nonbounded nature of this second clause makes it difficult to determine its relationship to the present tense clause: the two might overlap or might represent distinct time periods. However, the second clause obviously represents a period of time in which the character referred to was in a state of readiness to make a certain sacrifice.

The distinction between the indirect style and the free indirect style appears to be that the latter does not necessarily use an embedded proposition following a verb of thought or speech. Imbs and Grévisse give examples from this category also shown in (54) (Henri de Montherlant, cited by Imbs 1960:95) and (55) (La Fontaine 1929:VII,3, cited by Grévisse 1980:834).

(54) *Le baron fut outré: Léon n'avait pas le sou, et il se permettait d'être insolent!*

The baron was outraged: Leon didn't **have** [IMP] a penny, but he **allowed himself** [IMP] to be insolent!

(55) *Des députés du peuple rat/ s'en vinrent demander quelque aumône légère:/ ils allaient en terre étrangère/ chercher quelques secours contre le peuple chat.*

Some deputies from the rat people/ came [PS] to demand a few alms:/ They **were going** [IMP] into a foreign land/ to look for some assistance against the cat people.

Some examples of this usage are difficult to distinguish from commentary, so similar are the two in certain areas. Example (56), taken from Leblanc (1967:163) could be seen as either free indirect style or commentary.

(56) *Aurélie les regardaient avec horreur, mais ne bougeait pas. Tous deux étaient ses ennemis, pareillement exécrables.*

Aurelie watched with horror but didn't move. Both [of them] **were** [IMP] her enemies, equally abominable.

In all of these cases, the imparfait is used to represent a nonbounded state, which can be symbolized by —.

5.8. Picturesque, historical, or narrative. Perhaps the most intriguing occurrence of the imparfait is its use by some authors as a narrative tense rivalling the passé simple. Imbs (1960:92) and others state that the effect of this use is to describe and recount actions at the same time. Grévisse treats this as a particular use of the imparfait, deserving special mention as in (57) (J. Lemaitre, *Jean Racine*, p.118, cited by Grévisse 1980:834).

(57) *Donc tout réussissait à Racine. A vingt-cinq ans il entrait dans la renommée.*

Thus everything was succeeding for Racine. At the age of twenty-five, he **was entering** [IMP] into renown.

The effect of this replacement of the passé simple by the imparfait also seems to be a greater sense of immediacy: the reader is somehow there with the experiencer. It is as if one were saying "at this exact point in time, this was the state of affairs," as if the moment were prolonged or frozen before the eyes of the reader.

This quality of the imparfait has been mentioned by several authors who have cited the old description of the imparfait as the "present in the past." The imparfait has been characterized this way due to its resemblance to the present tense. This resemblance is described by Martin (1971:94):

At eight o'clock, he was having lunch signifies that at a precise moment in time a part of the process is seen as accomplished and another part is seen as not yet accomplished; the imparfait is a complex mechanism that offers an analytical view, discriminating in itself what is from what is not yet, artificially creating in the past a distinction that in fact is only true of the present.

Martin (1971:96) adds:

The durative-imperfective aspect [of the imparfait] . . . creates the illusion of a past still living, and this grammatical time seems to confer on the speaker the power to evoke, as if they were still in process, as if they were still unfolding, processes that, in fact, have long since been accomplished.

The reason for this effect is again the nonboundedness imparted by the imparfait. The trigger for such a use of the imparfait is the state-like qualities—of duration or 'sameness', continuity—that the author perceives in the situation. By choosing the imparfait, he is creating a state of affairs that held for the moment evoked and perhaps for some time before or after.

For this reason, the imparfait is a natural tense in which to report situations which were experienced during an altered state of consciousness. The author's experience is an important part of the account and this must be characterized even as the HAPPENINGS are recounted. The following excerpt from a dream seems to be an example of this (Victor Hugo, *Choses vues*, 14 déc 1842, cited by Imbs 1960:92).

(58) *Tout cet ensemble avait je ne sais quelle sérénité inexprimable. Il semblait qu'on y sentit l'âme des choses. J'invitais le prince à contempler cette belle nuit, et je me souviens que je lui disais distinctement ces paroles:—Vous êtes prince; on vous apprendra à admirer la politique humaine; apprenez à admirer la nature.*

All of this as a whole had [IMP] I don't know what inexpressible serenity. It seemed [IMP] that one could feel in it the very essence of things. I **was inviting** [IMP] the prince to contemplate the beautiful night, and I remember that I **was telling** [IMP] him distinctly these words, "You are a prince. They will teach you to appreciate human politics; teach yourself to appreciate nature."

Again, we see that what appears at first to be a peculiar or anomalous usage of the imparfait is explainable in terms of the defining value of the form: nonboundedness. The configuration for this use of the imparfait is again —.

5.9. Closing or opening. A usage of the imparfait which Imbs, though not Grévisse, distinguishes from the imparfait picturesque is the imparfait of closing (*rupture* or *clôture*). The imparfait of opening (*ouverture*), mentioned by Imbs, seems to be similar. This latter occurs at the beginning of a narrative and gives the first event as in (59) (Victor Hugo, cited by Imbs 1960:90).

(59) *Dans les premiers jours du mois d'octobre 1815, une heure avant le coucher du soleil, un homme qui voyageait à pied entrait dans la petite ville de Digne.*

In the first days of the month of October 1815, an hour before sunset, a man who was travelling on foot **entered** [IMP] the little town of Digne.

The imparfait of closing, on the other hand, occurs at the end of a narrative or episode. Imbs gives the examples in (60) (Victor Hugo, *Les Misérables,* cited by Imbs 1960:93) and (61) (Alexandre Dumas père, *Les Trois Mousquétaires,* vol. 2, chap. V, cited by Imbs 1960:93).

(60) *Le jour suivant, personne au Luxembourg. Marius attendit tout le jour puis alla faire sa faction de nuit sous les croisées. Cela le* **conduisait** *jusqu'à* **dix heures du soir.** *Son dîner* **devenait** *ce qu'il pouvait.*

The next day, [there was] no one at the Luxembourg. Marius waited all day and then went to do his nightly guard duty under the transcepts. That **took** him up [IMP] to **ten o'clock.** His dinner **became** [IMP] whatever he could get.

(61) *D'un autre côté, comme l'avait prévu Athos, Milady* ... *pensa qu'il valait mieux garder le silence, partir discrètement, accomplir avec son habileté ordinaire la mission difficile dont elle s'était chargée, puis toutes ces choses accomplies à la satisfaction du cardinal, venir lui réclamer sa vengeance.*

En conséquence, après avoir voyagé tout la nuit, à sept heures du matin elle **était embarquée,** *et à neuf heures le bâtiment, qui, avec des lettres de marque du cardinal, était censé être en partance pour Bayonne,* **levait** *l'ancre et* **faisait** *voile pour l'Angleterre.*

On the other hand, as Athos had foreseen, Milady ... **thought** that it would be ... better to keep quiet, to leave discreetly, to accomplish with her usual cleverness the difficult mission that she had taken on, then, all these things accomplished to the cardinal's satisfaction, to come back and claim her vengeance.

As a result, after having travelled all night, at seven o'clock in the morning, she **was** [IMP] **on board,** and at nine o'clock the vessel, which, with the cardinal's letters, was supposed to be parting for Bayonne, **was lifting** [IMP] its anchor and **hoisting** its sail for England.

Imbs describes this use of the imparfait as "presenting events as states in which the narrator sees the heros installed, and characterizing the final atmosphere of the drama" (Imbs 1960:93). Thus again the use of the imparfait can be considered to be state and to play a role similar to that which usually is found at the beginning of a narrative.

In a sense, the imparfait of opening and the imparfait of closing present scenes or snapshots of states. It is as if the curtain rises on an action already in progress and falls while it is still continuing. The imparfait does have the ability to present phenomena that are actually frozen in time, such as photographs or letters. The examples in (62) (Sartre, cited by Imbs 1960:91) and (63) (Dumas fils, 1983:70) demonstrate this use.

(62) *Il ouvrit le journal à la treizieme page! Gomez vit une photo: La Guardia serrait la main d'un gros homme, tous deux souriaient avec abandon.*

He opened the journal to the thirteenth page! Gomez saw a photo: La Guardia **was shaking** [IMP] the hand of a fat man, both of them **were smiling** [IMP] with abandon.

(63) *Le lendemain, au matin, je reçus une lettre de Duval, qui m'informait de son retour, et me priait de passer chez lui . . .*

The next day I received a letter from Duval, which **informed** [IMP] me of his return, and **begged** [IMP] me to come by his house.

A letter or a photo is unchanging and thus represents a state. The men in the photo smile continuously and their action, crystallized into a state, is presented to us at one particular moment of its duration in time. The images presented by the imparfait of opening and the imparfait of closing seem similarly frozen in time. Example (64) (Camus 1947:32–33) showing the imparfait of closing seems to demonstrate this.

(64) *—Ecoutez, dit [Rieux], il faut l'isoler et tenter un traitement d'exception. Je téléphone à l'hôpital et nous le transporterons en ambulance.*

Deux heures après, dans l'ambulance, le docteur et la femme se penchaient sur le malade. De sa bouche tapissée de fongosités, des bribes de mots sortaient: «Les rats!» disait-il. Verdâtre, les lèvres cireuses . . . le concierge étouffait sous une pesée invisible. La femme pleurait.

"Listen," said [Rieux], "we will need to isolate him and try a special treatment. I'll telephone the hospital and we'll transport him by ambulance."

Two hours later, in the ambulance, the doctor and the wife **were leaning** [IMP] over the sick man. From his mouth overgrown with fungi **were coming** [IMP] fragments of words: "The rats!," he **was saying** [IMP]. Greenish in color, his lips waxen... the caretaker **was smothering** [IMP] under an invisible weight. His wife was **crying** [IMP].

5.10. Habitual. This use is attested by Imbs, Grévisse, and Lasserre and Grandjean. Imbs gives the examples in (65) and (66) (Balzac 1973:28–30 cited by Imbs 1960:96).

(65) *Généralement, les pensionnaires externes ne s'abonnaient qu'au dîner.*

Generally, the outside tenants only **signed up** [IMP] for dinners.

(66) *Outre les sept pensionnaires internes, Madame Vauquer avait bon an mal an huit étudiants en droit ou en médecine.*

In addition to the seven live-in tenants, Madame Vauquer **had** [IMP], in good years as in bad, eight students in law or in medicine.

It is interesting to note that in both of these examples, there is an adverbial of time that denotes iterativity: *généralement* 'generally' and *bon an mal an* 'in good years as in bad'. If such a modifier could be identified in the context of each habitual use of the imparfait, one could classify it as a marked use. An imparfait which was not marked in this way would thus be understood to have merely continuative but not iterative meaning.

Why would the imparfait—a tense of continuous uninterrupted action— be used to convey an iterative situation?

The answer may lie in a relationship, noted by Vendler (1967), between states and habitual action. In his treatment of verb types, Vendler (1967:108) describes the association between the two types of situations in the following way:

Habits (in a broader sense including occupations, dispositions, abilities, and so forth) are also states in our sense. Compare the two questions: Are you smoking? and Do you smoke? The first one asks about an activity, the second, a state. This difference explains why a chess player can say at all times that he plays chess and why a worker for the General Electric Company can say, while sunbathing on the beach, that he works for General Electric.

An activity that is continual, that becomes characteristic, thus becomes a state. This can be seen in (67), which contains only imparfait verb forms. Although almost all of these predicates are dynamic, the paragraph is a description passage, characterizing a period of time, rather than an action passage (Flaubert 1972:93).

(67) *Charles, à la neige à la pluie, chevauchait par les chemins de traverse. Il mangeait des omelettes sur la table des fermes, entrait son bras dans des lits humides, recevait au visage le jet tiède des saignées, écoutait des râles, examinait des cuvettes, retroussait bien du linge sale; mais il trouvait, tous les soirs, un feu flambant, la table servie, des meubles souples, et une femme en toilette fine, charmante et sentant frais...*

Charles, come rain come snow, **rode** his horse over the back roads. He **ate** omelets at farmhouse tables, **put** his arm into damp beds, **was hit** in the face by spurting blood during bleedings, **listened to** death rattles, **examined** washbasins, **rolled back** a great deal of dirty linen; but every evening he **found** a flaming fire, a table already set, comfortable chairs and a well-groomed, charming, sweet-smelling wife...

Although each of these situations can be seen as a configuration of ···· or ----, the fact that they are characteristic, that they dominate a period of time, causes them to be seen as —.

5.11. Progression. Imbs gives examples of this type of use, which he sees as "being only a variety of duration" (Alexandre Dumas père 1943:247; J. Green, cited by Imbs 1960:96).

(68) *... à mesure qu'il s'avançait en entrant dans la cercle de lumière projeté par la lampe, Milady se reculait involontairement.*

As he **moved further and further forward** into the circle of light projected by the lamp, Milady involuntarily **drew further and further back.**

(69) *Plus il y réfléchissait, plus il lui paraissait évident que la morte vivait de nouveau dans le corps de sa fille.*

The more he **thought** about it, **the more** it seemed obvious to him that the dead woman lived again in the body of his daughter.

The habitual or iterative examples that we examined earlier had lexical markings that indicated their habituality. In the same way, these examples have lexical markings and structures that indicate their progressiveness.

Another type of example, with explanation, is given by Grévisse in (70) (Michelet, Hist. de la Révol. fr., II, 2; Bibliothéque de la Pléiade, t. I, p.183, cited by Grévisse 1980:834).

(70) *Un imparfait de progression, marqué par la périphrase allait + participe présent: L'impôt **allait** pesant sur une terre toujours plus pauvre.*

An imparfait of progression, marked by the paraphrase 'was going' + the present participle: "The tax **was going weighing** [i.e., was weighing more and more] on an ever poorer land."

The concept of progression can also be expressed by the verb or predicate used as in (71) (Flaubert 1972:100).

(71) *Emma **devenait** difficile, capricieuse.*

Emma **was becoming** difficult, capricious.

What seems clear is that progressiveness is not a value that derives from the imparfait itself but from the continuousness associated with the imparfait plus some other factor.

In summary, we have thus seen that each of these various uses for the imparfait illustrates its core value: nonboundedness. Each creates the sense of a state or a state of affairs.

5.12–5.13 Passé simple: Uses

5.12. Nonstative verbs. Nonstative verbs, particularly those with a high or marked degree of dynamicity, can be considered the natural clients of the passé simple. As Reid has noted, dynamic verbs are statistically most likely to be encoded in the passé simple. Placed in a series, they form a fast moving and dynamic account (Leblanc 1967:6–7).

(72) *Elle **traversa** la place de l'Opéra, sans se soucier des véhicules qui l'encombraient. Un camion **voulut** lui barrer le passage : posément elle **saisit** les rênes du cheval et l'**immobilisa**. Furieux, le conducteur **sauta** de son siège et l'**injuria** de trop près; elle lui **décocha** sur le nez un petit coup de poing qui **fit** jaillir le sang. Un agent de police*

réclama des explications : elle lui tourna le dos et s'éloigna paisiblement.

She **crossed** the square of the Opera, with no concern for the vehicles that were encumbering it. A truck **tried** to bar her route. Calmly she **seized** the horse's reins and **immobilized** it. Furious, the conductor **jumped** down from his seat and, moving too close, **insulted** her; she **struck** him a little blow to the nose that made it spurt blood. A policeman **demanded** an explanation: she **turned** her back on him and calmly **walked away**.

In (72) we have an impression of quick action. The whole episode might take no more than a minute or two. This is one of the effects of the passé simple: to give such an impression of dynamicity by a chain of what are, unquestionably, events.

On the other hand, the passé simple, as Comrie has noted, is not limited to punctiliar events (Flaubert 1972:151).

(73) *Emma maigrit, ses joues pâlirent, sa figure s'allongea.*

Emma **became thin,** her cheeks **paled,** her face **grew longer.**

Obviously this situation lasted longer than five minutes.

5.13. Stative verbs. The use of stative verbs with the passé simple is more unusual, but not infrequent. As we have seen, even the most stative of verbs, *être,* can and frequently is used in the passé simple.

This is one type of perfective that Comrie does not place in terms of event or state. He gives examples of Russian and Greek perfective forms of stative verbs, characterizes these as referring "not only to the state obtaining at a given time, but also to its inception and termination" and admits that these thus "do include a dynamic element." However, he characterizes the occurrence of stative verbs with perfective meanings as rare and as having a "rather restricted semantic range" (1976:50). Unfortunately, Comrie overlooks the frequency of this type of construction in French.

The definition of the passé simple that we have been developing over the past few chapters would suggest that the passé simple is used in two ways: (1) redundantly—when a concept of boundedness is already explicit in a predicate; and, (2) nonredundantly—when the speaker or writer wishes to add a concept of boundedness to a predicate that does not have explicit boundaries.

This boundedness may have one or more possible interpretations. Generally, when a speaker encounters a verb that is strongly marked in terms of boundedness in a nonredundant aspect, he is forced to determine the meaning by deduction. To do this, he must rely on his knowledge of the language as well as the context of the usage, given the notion of boundedness that has been added.

Abrate recognizes this ambiguity in her comments on nonmomentary verbs that occur in the imparfait. In her view, the passé simple may be used with nonmomentary verbs to add one of two ideas to the predicate: termination or momentariness (Abrate 1983:549).

She illustrates this with the sentence *j'ai connu son frère* 'I knew his brother'. Since *connaître* 'to know, to be acquainted with' fits into her classification as a nonmomentary verb, the use of it in the passé simple must imply an element of either termination 'I once knew his brother' or momentariness 'I met his brother'. Abrate notes that "context is of primary importance in determining the implied meaning" (p. 549).

Abrate's use of the term 'momentariness' here can also have the sense of what Cox has identified as inception: 'I met' can also mean 'I began to know'. Thus it appears that there are these three possibilities: the boundary can be at the beginning, or at the end, or it can encompass the whole of the state or action.

Let us turn to the relationship between these bounded stative verbs and event and state as defined in chapter three. Three different types of examples are examined and placed in relation to event.

The first and perhaps most common instance of a stative verb in the passé simple pertains only to *être* 'to be'. This form of *être* plus a past participle frequently indicates a passive passé simple construction as shown in (74) (Aymé 1943:81–82).

(74) *Enfin, par l'entremise du Vatican, un accord international fut conclu qui délivrait les peuples du cauchemar de la guerre sans rien changer à l'issue normale des hostilités.*

Finally, through the intervention of the Vatican, an international accord **was concluded** [PS] that delivered the people from the nightmare of the war, without changing at all the normal outcome of the hostilities.

What is presented here is obviously an event; it is the passive counterpart of *on conclut un accord international* 'they concluded an international accord'. The passé simple form of *être* is thus handy for distinguishing an event from a state (such as *un accord international était conclu*) in a way not possible in English.

Second, the passé simple of *être* can also be used in a skewed sentence, that is, in a sentence where a clause with a typical event verb or situation is embedded in a clause with a stative one. The function of the passé simple *être* in such a sentence seems to be to agree with the subordinate verb in the feature of boundedness and thus signal that an event did indeed take place. An example of this usage is seen in (75) (Flaubert 1965:159).

(75) *Ce fut quinze jours après que Liébard, à l'heure du marché, comme d'habitude, **entra** dans la cuisine, et lui **remit** une lettre qu'envoyait son beau-frère.*

It **was** [PS] fifteen days after, that Liébard, at the market hour, as was his habit, **came into** [PS] the kitchen and **gave** [PS] her a letter sent by her brother.

Thus a construction containing an embedded event proposition is marked as an event proposition.

Third, we often find that a passé simple form of a stative verb presents a state which has claims to being an event. The condition that it describes either (a) lasted the same amount of time as a contiguous event proposition; or (b) was short and intense and thus resembles an event. The sentence in (76) is an example of (a), simultaneity with an event, that we examined earlier (Pagnol 1985:38).

(76) *Il fut poli et discret. Sans mot dire, il glissa jusqu'au bout du siège, et tira près de lui son chapeau melon.*

He **was** [PS] polite and discreet. Without a word, he slid all the way to the end of the bench and pulled his bowler hat next to him.

This is a use of *être* in the passé simple which is very frequently used by some writers. Its [+ bounded] feature allows it to be used to characterize an action or a specified period of time in the story and it often seems to bear the same relation to *être* in the imparfait as the two 'be' verbs, *estar* and *ser*, bear to one another in Spanish.

The meaning of (76) is that the man **acted** discreetly and politely, making room for others on his bench. The politeness and discretion referred to had the same duration as the events (his sliding to the end of the bench and pulling his hat out of the way).

An example of a short, intense condition, to illustrate (b) above, is seen in (77) (Dumas fils 1983:89).

(77) *Je compris le mal que j'avais dû lui faire par celui que j'éprouvais, et pendant cinq minutes je l'**aimai** comme jamais on n'aima une femme.*

I understood the pain that I had caused her by that which I was feeling and for five minutes I **loved** [PS] her as no one ever loved a woman.

Here *aimai* 'loved' is short and intense. It has a duration of only five minutes and its qualifiers, 'as no one ever loved a woman', show that it has uncommon power. It thus has the force of an event. In this instance, the time modifier *pendant cinq minutes* 'for five minutes' makes it clear that the boundary encompasses the whole of the action. In other cases, the verb *aimer* in the passé simple can have the sense of inception 'began to love.'

We see in all of the above examples that the passé simple represents event, an idea of boundedness. This is even true when the verb is a stative one: by the use of the passé simple, it is being made into an event. This boundedness may have three possible interpretations: inception, momentariness, or termination.

6

Event and State in a French
Narrative Text

In chapter two, we briefly examined the foregrounding and backgrounding approach to the passé simple and the imparfait. Advocates of this
approach assert that foregrounding/backgrounding in discourse represents
a basic function of the passé simple/imparfait opposition with some main-
taining that it represents the only function of the passé simple/imparfait
opposition. On the basis of a textual analysis, however, it can be contended
(1) that the passé simple has a basic meaning of event and the imparfait
has a basic meaning of state, and (2) that all discourse functions of these
two tenses are based on these meanings.

Weinrich was one of the first to study the functions of the passé simple
and the imparfait at a discourse level and perhaps the first to formulate
these in terms of a foregrounding/backgrounding approach. He states
categorically that the foregrounding/backgrounding function "is the sole
and unique function of the opposition between Imparfait and Passé simple
in the narrated world" (Weinrich 1973:116).

The phrase, "in the narrated world," may appear to limit the scope of
Weinrich's claim. However, such is not the case. Weinrich's theory of
tense/aspect divides all human speech into two categories: the "commented
world," in which the speaker is personally involved in what he is relating,
and the "narrated world," in which he is relating events that are removed
from him. Weinrich then assigns all tenses to one or the other of these
worlds but never to both. The passé simple and imparfait tenses are both
assigned to the narrated world. Thus we see that Weinrich's statement
amounts to a claim that foregrounding/backgrounding is the only existing
function of the passé simple/imparfait opposition.

It appears that Weinrich is correct concerning the passé simple and the imparfait having discourse level functions, and about the passé simple/imparfait opposition corresponding, in narrative, to a distinction between foreground and background. However, he may not be correct about the binary narrative/commentary division of discourse and also about the passé simple and imparfait having no discourse functions other than the foregrounding/backgrounding opposition.

In the preceding chapters, it has been shown that the defining characteristic of the passé simple is boundedness and of the imparfait is nonboundedness. It has been demonstrated that these concepts, in turn, can be related to those of event and state, which would constitute the basic meanings of the two tenses. It is left now to show that these meanings can account for all the occurrences of the imparfait and the passé simple in a discourse. Furthermore, these meanings underlie the foregrounding/backgrounding function of the passé simple/imparfait opposition in narrative discourse as well as other functions of these two tenses in other types of discourse. An analysis of a narrative text, "L'huissier" by Marcel Aymé, is used to demonstrate this thesis in terms of its use of the passé simple and the imparfait. This text is narrative in the main but has some embedding of other discourse types within it, and will help to demonstrate that an event versus state opposition explains not only the structuring of the narrative as a whole but also the structure of nonnarrative paragraphs and segments found within the text.

The method of analysis is basically that of Longacre, as it has been set forth in various works (1981; 1983). Longacre posits two levels of analysis for a text: the surface structure and the underlying or notional structure which motivates that text. Furthermore, he has set forth a classification of discourse types based on two parameters: agent orientation and contingent temporal succession. The interaction of these two parameters yields four different classifications as in (78) (Longacre 1983:5).[10]

Agent oriented texts can be contrasted with theme oriented texts, such as scientific papers. Contingent temporal succession "refers to a framework ... in which some (often most) of the events or doings are contingent on previous events or doings" (Longacre 1983:3).

---

[10]Longacre (1983:5) also posits two additional parameters: projection and tension, which make further distinctions within these classifications.

(78)   A typology of discourse texts

	+Agent orientation	−Agent orientation
+Contingent temporal succession	narrative	procedural
−Contingent temporal succession	hortatory	expository

6.1–6.8 Surface structure of "L'huissier"

In the surface structure analysis, the text is broken down into its con-stituent parts and then examined and compared for the use of the imparfait and the passé simple within each of these parts. The analysis is limited to independent clause predicates which are external to the dialogue portions of the text. As the imparfait is less frequent and has a more limited distribution within the text than the passé simple, special focus is placed on examples of its use.

6.1. Initial chunking of "L'huissier." A first division can be made in the text by consulting two very basic plot concerns: the physical setting of the action (the location) and the participants. This yields a four-part division as shown in (79).

(79)

Surface slot	Sentences	Participants	Location
Stage	1	Malicorne	French town
Episode 1	2–80	Malicorne, Saint Peter, God	Heaven
Episode 2	81–216	Malicorne, his wife, his clerk, Gorgerin, others	French town
Episode 3	217–233	Malicorne, Saint Peter, God	Heaven

The most obvious feature shown in this chart is the "sandwich" effect of episodes 1, 2, and 3. Episode 2 clearly contrasts with episodes 1 and 3, which are parallel sections. These two sections also share an organizing "script" that could be entitled "judgment after death."

A further structural indication that episodes 1 and 2 are distinct is the preposed adverbial clauses found in sentences[11] 2 and 81, examples (80) and (81). These two introducers form a perfect pair in terms of time, location, and participant reference.

(80) *Une nuit qu'il reposait auprès de sa femme, Malicorne...* (S2)

One night as he was sleeping next to his wife, Malicorne...

(81) *Le lendemain en s'éveillant auprès de son épouse, Malicorne...* (S81)

The next day upon awakening next to his spouse, Malicorne...

Grimes (1975:51) states that "where, when, and under what circumstances actions take place constitute a separate kind of information structure called SETTING." Longacre (1983:xvii) uses the term "stage" for this type of introduction to a narrative. These concepts seem very similar to the nonbounded "state of affairs" defined earlier. It can be seen then that the relationship of these clauses to what follows is that of state of affairs to event or events. On a discourse level, we would say that they are providing a stage or setting for the episodes that follow.

It is interesting to note two other details of correspondence between these two clauses: (1) the verbal parallelism of *reposait* 'was resting' and *en s'éveillant* 'in awakening', and (2) the use of the synonyms *sa femme* 'his wife' and *son épouse* 'his spouse'. These parallel adverbial clauses set off episode 1, which constitutes a complete embedded narrative in itself.

The fact that the author has chosen to use two time-markers of this specification: specific time + specific location, specific participant to introduce two main divisions of the text indicates that it is a device that might occur marking other key breakdowns of the text. One might expect that episode 3 would begin with a similar device; however, such is not the case. Episode 3 does not have a preposed introducer. This seems at first somewhat asymmetrical, but, from the standpoint of the storyline, it is easy to understand. Such an introducer is not necessary here. The script that governs the transition from episode 2 to episode 3 has already been defined in the movement from the stage to episode 1, thus an introduction would be redundant.

One can compare this rough breakdown into these four sections with a tally of verb forms such as the following. I have used only the independent

---

[11]Sentence numbers refer to the glossed text in the appendix and are indicated by S followed by the sentence number in parentheses.

clause verbs (dialogue sections are excluded) and have divided these into three categories according to tense/aspect: passé simple, imparfait, and "other" (which includes plus-que-parfaits and modals).

(82)   Surface slot   Passé simple   Imparfait   Other

	Passé simple	Imparfait	Other
Stage	1	2	1
Episode 1	25	4	2
Episode 2	62	60	10
Episode 3	9	1	0
Total	97	67	13

This configuration shows an interesting correspondence to the patterns we have seen above in that the passé simple is shown to have a much higher frequency of use in episodes 1 and 3 than in episode 2. In episode 2, not only does the number of imparfait tense verbs rise to rival the total of passé simple forms, but the latter is less than the total of the two other categories together. In episodes 1 and 3, on the other hand, the passé simple forms outnumber all the imparfait forms at a ratio of 6 to 1 and 9 to 1 respectively. The sandwich effect shown by the participant and location structures is thus reflected in the overall distribution of verb tenses.

Although a certain amount of variation might be expected in the ratio of foreground to background clauses within a discourse, variation to this degree seems to suggest a basic change, or changes, in the discourse type. In fact, we find that episodes 1 and 3 are straight narrative sections, while episode 2 contains non-narrative as well as narrative portions.

Since episodes 1 and 3 are relatively homogeneous and have fewer imparfait forms, I begin with these, leaving episode 2, which presents more complexities, until last.

6.2. Episode 1. Episode 1 (S2–80) is characterized by dialogue and by a virtual absence of tenses other than the passé simple. As shown in (82), there are 25 passé simple forms, 4 imparfait forms (S28, 35, 65, 74) and 2 "other" forms (S32, 75).

A reading of the passé simple forms shows that these are all bounded events that succeed one another chronologically, i.e., that are in contingent temporal succession. As events, or bounded situations, are used to establish a contingent temporal succession, bounded events thus correlate with foreground.

The four imparfait forms are examined individually and related to the contexts in which they occur to determine the meanings and functions.

Episode 1 can be described as a judgment scene. The dialogue and actions are recounted entirely in the passé simple up until Saint Peter's sentence is pronounced. Then, all of a sudden, we have sentence 28.

(83) *Déjà les anges se précipitaient.*   (S28)

Already the angels were descending.

Up until this point, the sentences have succeeded one another in an orderly fashion, much as points on a line. Then suddenly there is one which slides under its predecessor with this little word *déjà* 'already'. The action of the angels has begun during the previous action, which is a speech act: while Saint Peter was still speaking, the angels began their descent.

This is the imparfait that many have called "simultaneous," i.e., "not sequential." It effortlessly slides under the preceding action. How does it do this? It is able to do it because it is not bounded—it lacks a beginning boundary in time.

The next sentence, S29, makes it clear that the imparfait in sentence 28 also lacks a terminative boundary.

(84) *Malicorne les arrêta d'un geste très ferme.*   (S29)

Malicorne stopped them with a very firm gesture.

At the beginning of Malicorne's action, the angels are still descending; his action interrupts their downward motion and thus creates a terminative boundary for it. The nonboundedness of sentence 28 thus has the result we have seen earlier: it becomes a state of affairs that is interrupted by an event.

The next imparfait example follows the entrance of God into the story as a participant:

(85) *Lui non plus ne paraissait pas avoir les huissiers en grande faveur.* (S35)

He didn't seem to hold bailiffs in any great favor either.

This is another simultaneous sentence, in this case describing a state which is true of the character throughout this episode. As God entered the scene, it was clear to all that his attitude toward bailiffs was not favorable. This attitude was not momentary; it continued and influenced his actions, as is shown by the passé simple sentence in (86). The imparfait in sentence 35 thus encodes a nonbounded state.

(86) *On le vit bien à sa façon bourrue d'interroger Malicorne.* (S36)

One saw this clearly in his brusque/gruff way of questioning Malicorne.

Further along there is a very interesting sentence in the passé simple:

(87) *Il fut trop facile de vérifier que ces belles paroles ne cachaient aucune bonne action, ni aucune bonne pensée dont une âme ne pût prévaloir devant le tribunal suprême.* (S64)

It was too easy to establish that these pretty words didn't hide any good deed or any good thought by which a soul might prevail before the supreme tribunal.

We would expect a sentence that begins, "It was too easy," to use the imparfait; however, the verb *être* here is in the passé simple. The reason for this is the infinitive *vérifier*. What the author is communicating is that an event, verification, did take place. The sentence, *Il était trop facile de vérifier que . . .*, 'It was [IMP] too easy to verify that . . .' would imply that the state of things was such at this time that verification would have been easy but that it was not, in fact, carried out.[12] The difference in these two tenses here is the boundary that is communicated by the passé simple and that tells the reader that an event did in fact occur.

The sentence that follows this one is:

(88) *Dieu paraissait très contrarié.* (S65)

God appeared to be very irritated.

His irritation results from the preceding interview (in which Malicorne has failed to remember any good deeds) and the instant verification of Malicorne's poor record by Heaven's own files. The result of this irritation is a tongue-lashing by God of Saint Peter which takes place in the next sentence. Thus the appearance of God's irritation has no clear beginning boundary nor ending boundary but it 'slides under' both the preceding and the following actions, and thus represents a state that lasted some time.

The next sentence (S74) marks the final imparfait in this section. Saint Peter was keeping silent during God's tongue-lashing, and he continues to do so as God waits for an answer and then speaks again. Sentence 74 is thus another example of a state.

---

[12]In a different context, *Il était facile de vérifier* might mean that verification was something that was commonly done, e.g., by a number of people over a certain period of time. In this case, it would still give the sense of a state or a state of affairs.

(89) *Saint Pierre gardait un silence maussade.*   (S74)

Saint Peter was sullenly keeping silent.

(90) *Le laissant à sa mauvaise humeur, Dieu se tourna vers Malicorne*
et lui dit en bon français...   (S76)

Leaving him to his bad mood, God turned to Malicorne and said
to him in good French...

Thus, all of the imparfaits in this section represent states or states of
affairs and they classify as background information that is secondary to the
narrative. The passé simple forms, on the other hand, all represent events
and are sequenced in such a way that each depends on the completion of
the preceding event. Therefore, event and state correlate with the functions of foregrounding and backgrounding.

6.3. Episode 3. Episode 3 (S217–233) consists of nine passé simple constructions and one imparfait. The nine passé simple forms, of which three
are speech acts, clearly occur in succession. One of these forms (S225) uses
the verb *vouloir* 'want, want to', which is generally classified as a verb of
state. However, this bounded passé simple form has the meaning of
'wanted to and attempted to'. This is thus an example of a predicate that
has both a bounded and a non-bounded sense. (See §4.6)

The one imparfait construction in this short section is S217. By virtue of
its placement at the beginning of this section, this imparfait clause can be
identified as a setting. It presents the location and the state of affairs for
the episode that will follow.

(91) *Dieu se trouvait à passer par la salle d'audience, lorsque*
Malicorne fut admis à comparaître.   (S217)

God happened to be passing by the audience hall when
Malicorne was admitted for arraignment.

An interrupting action, in the passé simple, is presented in a subordinate
clause of the same sentence. The configuration of this imparfait is thus that
of the so-called classic opposition of the imparfait and passé simple: ——●
(see §5.3) which represents a state of affairs interrupted by an event.

6.4. Breakdown of episode 2. This episode is much longer and more
complex than the two just examined. Whereas episodes 1 and 3 contained
only imparfait forms, passé simple forms, and speech acts (with the exception of one present tense verb and one hypothetical construction of

indirect speech in episode 1), episode 2 contains a wide variety of other tenses. To make such complexity manageable, episode 2 is considered in smaller chunks, as listed in (92).

(92) Surface slot   Sentences

    Episode 2a   81–156
    Episode 2b1   157–185
    Episode 2b2   186–216

The first types of dividers to look for are those which we have already found marking major divisions of the story. In fact, another introducer of the type that sets off episode 1 is found inside episode 2 at sentence 157.

(93) *Un matin qu'il venait de saisir les meubles d'un chômeur, l'huissier, tandis qu'il marchait par les ruelles du bas quartier, ...*

                                                                     (S157)

One morning as he had just seized the furniture of an un-employed man, the bailiff, while he was walking through the alleys of the lower quarter, ...

That this is another specific time + specific location + participant marker is immediately apparent. As in S2 and S81, the author gives not only a specific time reference but also a location (the alleys of the lower quarter) and a particular participant (Malicorne again), as well as the ongoing activity that he was involved in (walking). He also places his participant in terms of the activity that he has just completed (seizing the furniture of an unemployed man).

The time adverbial *un matin* 'one morning' is significant as it occurs after a long period of increasingly vague time reference (moving from 'the day after [his resurrection]' to 'the next day and the days that followed' to 'in four months' to 'at the end of a year'). It thus represents a significant narrowing of the time margin; in a sense, the story clock has just started ticking again.

We have seen that this type of introductory clause serves as setting at the beginning of episodes 1 and 2. Thus, the clause in S157 seems to introduce a new episode which would qualify as a second division of episode 2. In fact, sentences 157–216 appear to represent one long em-bedded episode, much like episode 1 or episode 3.

Later in episode 2 (at sentence 186), there is another time reference: the punctiliar adverb *soudain* 'suddenly'. This preposed adverb describes the dramatic entrance of M. Gorgerin onto the scene.

In terms of overall ranking of participants in episode 2, it is evident that the antagonist, Gorgerin, is second in importance only to Malicorne, the protagonist. In both of his appearances, Gorgerin speaks, expressing opinions and intentions, and, at the end of episode 2, he kills Malicorne.

Thus, his re-entrance onto the stage in sentence 186, just preceding his confrontation with Malicorne, appears to mark the beginning of a new section of the text. Although such a division represents a break not only within an episode but within a paragraph as well, the use of *soudain* and the accompanying change in pace, which characterizes the remainder of episode 2, seem indicative of a new section.

The author's orthographic paragraphing needs to be challenged here, as it was challenged at the beginning of the text where a division was made in the first paragraph. The first paragraph of "L'huissier" contains a one-sentence stage as well as a second sentence that belongs to episode 1. This division between episode 2b1 and episode 2b2 seems to be similar enough to constitute a single episode with episode 2b1 serving as a stage for episode 2b2. This division is not the same sort that separates episode 1 from episode 2 or episode 2a from episodes 2b1 and 2b2. Episodes 2b1 and 2b2 are examined separately.

Episode 2 may be broken down into two divisions: sentences 81–156 and sentences 157–216, and the second division may be split into another two divisions: sentences 157–185 and sentences 186–216, to give a total of three sections as shown in (92).

In comparing the three sections of episode 2 in terms of verb forms, great diversity can be seen in the ratios of passé simple to imparfait forms. In 2a, the two are almost equally represented. In 2b1, imparfaits outnumber passé simples at a ratio of almost 2 to 1. Episode 2b2 resembles Episodes 1 and 3 in that passé simple forms outnumber imparfait forms, but the ratio of 3 to 1 is less dramatic than the 6 to 1 or 9 to 1 ratios of passé simple to imparfait forms in episodes 1 and 3. The distributing verb forms in episode 2 are listed in (94).

(94)	Surface slot	Passé simple	Imparfait	Other
	Episode 2a	34	32	5
	Episode 2b1	13	23	4
	Episode 2b2	15	5	1

In these sections, particular focus is again on the imparfait forms. Episodes 2b1 and 2b2 are broken down further in terms of their constituent units and then examined individually and as they relate to the whole. At least two levels of structure are analyzed in the sections: that of the overall section and that of each of the smaller units that compose a given section.

6.5. Episode 2a. Episode 2a is perhaps the most complex in terms of its structure. Although the passé simple forms are distributed throughout this section, most of the imparfaits occur towards the end. The reasons for this become clear as the structure of this episode is examined.

There might be two overall themes for this episode: 'buying salvation' and 'Malicorne's new reputation'. The first theme derives from the events in the last section, and eventually gives way to the second. The first theme can be found in the first sentence of this section, S81.

(95) *Le lendemain matin, en s'éveillant auprès de son épouse, Malicorne aurait pu croire qu'il avait rêvé, mais il ne s'y trompa point et réfléchit aux moyens de faire son salut.* (S81)

The next day upon awakening next to his wife, Malicorne might have thought that he had been dreaming, but he didn't make that mistake, and he **reflected on means of gaining his salvation**.

The theme of 'buying salvation' is reflected in the series of short action vignettes that describe how Malicorne spent that first day; see (96).

(96) action 1   gives raise to Bourrichon (S84–86)
      action 2   sets up notebook and records good deed (S87–93)
      action 3   receives visit from Gorgerin (S94–118)
      action 4   gives raise to Mélanie (S119–120)
      action 5   records good deed (S121–122)
      action 6   visits several poor families (S123–127)

The visit from Gorgerin may not seem to fit this theme; Malicorne uses the occasion, however, to try for one more good deed (talking Gorgerin out of ejecting some tenants), and he also gets his idea, from something Gorgerin says, of giving away money on a large scale.

Each of these vignettes is set off at the beginning by either a definite time reference, S94, 'around nine o'clock', or, more frequently, by a back-reference such as S119, 'after having accompanied his client to the door' and S123, 'having no one else to give a raise to'. In one instance, it is a sentence: S87, 'The expression of this gratitude did not move the heart of the bailiff'.

In these sections, the passé simple continues to dominate. The first independent clause imparfait forms mostly serve as settings for vignettes.

For example, the sentences which follow the theme sentence given above and immediately precede action 1 are S82–83.

(97) *Il y pensait* [IMP] *encore lorsqu'il pénétra dans son étude, à huit heures. Son clerc, le vieux Bourrichon, qui travaillait* [IMP] *avec lui depuis trente ans, était* [IMP] *déjà assis à sa table.*   (S82–83)

He was still thinking [IMP] about this when he entered his study at eight o'clock. His clerk, the old Bourrichon, who had worked [IMP] with him for thirty years, was [IMP] already seated at the table.

What he was still thinking about was a means of gaining his salvation. This sentence is presenting his state of mind. Bourrichon is also presented in terms of who he is in Malicorne's life and of his presence on this occasion. All three of these clauses represent states. The one event mentioned, Malicorne's entrance into his office, is in a dependent clause and is thus marked as subordinate.

A second setting is given with imparfait sentences at the beginning of action 3—Gorgerin's visit in S95–96.

(98) *C'était* [IMP] *un gros propriétaire possédant quarante-deux immeubles dans la ville, et que le défaut d'argent de certain de ses locataires obligeait à recourir très souvent au ministère de Malicorne. Cette fois, il venait* [IMP] *l'entretenir d'une famille besogneuse qui était en retard de deux termes.*   (S95–96)

This was [IMP] a stout landlord who owned forty-two buildings in the city and who was often obliged, by the negative financial status of some of his tenants, to make use of Malicorne's services. **This time**, he was coming [IMP] to see Malicorne about a needy family that was two terms late.

This is a two-part setting: first, Gorgerin himself is introduced in terms of his relation to Malicorne and in terms of the usual nature of his visits to Malicorne's office; then the specific nature of the visit is given. Thus, two types of setting are used for this vignette: general and specific.

The next imparfait form occurs in the paragraph following action 3 in S117–118. Again, this is an example like those examined earlier: a state of mind rather than an action.

(99) *Malicorne n'osa pas achever sa pensée. Il rêvait* [IMP] *à la situation confortable d'un pécheur arrivant devant le tribunal de Dieu précédé de la rumeur de toute une ville qui témoignait de sa bonté.*
(S117–118)

Malicorne did not dare complete his thought. He was dreaming [IMP] of the comfortable situation of a sinner arriving before the tribunal of God, preceded by the noise of a whole town that testified of his goodness.

A different type of imparfait occurs in action 6, S123–127.

(100) *N'ayant plus personne à augmenter, il s'en alla* [PS] *dans les bas quartiers de la ville, où il visita* **quelques familles pauvres**. *Les hôtes ne le voyaient pas* [IMP] *entrer sans appréhension et l'accueillaient* [IMP] *avec une réserve hostile, mais il se hâtait* [IMP] *de les rassurer et laissait en partant un billet de cinquante francs. En général, lorsqu'il était sorti, ses obligés empochaient* [IMP] *l'argent en grommelant:* «*Vieux voleur (ou vieil assassin, ou vieux grippe-sou), il peut bien faire la charité avec tout ce qu'il a gagné sur notre misère.*» *Mais c'était là plutôt une façon de parler qu'imposait la pudeur d'un revirement d'opinion.*   (S123–127)

Having no one else to give a raise to, he went down into the lower districts of the town and visited **several poor families**. It was with apprehension that his hosts watched [IMP] him enter their homes, and they greeted [IMP] him with hostile reserve, but he hastened [IMP] to reassure them and left [IMP] each time a fifty franc note. In general, when he had left, his benefactees pocketed the money, grumbling: "Old thief (or old murderer or old Scrooge), he can afford to give some away with all that he has gained from our misery." But then that was [IMP] the cautiousness that went with a sudden change of opinion.

This vignette is first recounted in the passé simple and then characterized in the imparfait. In essence, the imparfait sentences serve only to modify the passé simple sentence as a type of adverbial. The phrase 'several poor families' seems to serve as a trigger for the imparfait here because it provides a cue for a different type of action, i.e., repeated action. Because Malicorne is visiting several poor families, these separate but unquantified visits can be described together, as a procedure or ritual: Malicorne would do this and then his hosts would do this, etc. Thus, the imparfait here describes habitual action.

The fact that the imparfait forms here are habitual is not somehow inherent in the forms themselves but is determined by contextual elements, namely the 'several poor families' and the 'in general' of sentence 125. As we noted earlier (§5.10), habitual actions are related to states; they represent states of affairs. The final imparfait form is another author evaluation or commentary.

In these six vignettes, the imparfait represents state or state of affairs, and constitutes background. The passé simple, on the other hand, represents sequential events and carries the foreground.

There are two different levels of structure in episode 2a: the internal structures of the paragraphs themselves as well as the overall structure of the section. The widened time margin section consists of six orthographic paragraphs: sentences 128–131, 132–135, 136–140, 141–146, 147–152, and 153–156.

The first paragraph (S128–131) is one of the most difficult to analyze in terms of its structure and its mainline tense. It is introduced by a sentence in the plus-que-parfait tense.

(101) *Au soir de sa résurrection, Malicorne avait inscrit dans son cahier douze bonnes actions qui lui revenaient à six cent francs, et pas une mauvaise.*   (S128)

By the evening of his resurrection, Malicorne had recorded in his notebook twelve good deeds which cost him six hundred francs, and not one bad one.

This sentence seems to amount to a break in the timeline; we are now looking back at events which have already transpired from a timepoint a little further forward in the past. The next sentence is a return to the normal viewpoint.

(102) *Le lendemain et les jours suivants, il continua de distribuer de l'argent aux familles nécessiteuses.*   (S129)

The next day and in the days that followed, he continued to distribute money to needy families.

This appears to be a normal passé simple mainline sentence, summing up the action. It is followed, however, by another plus-que-parfait.

(103) *Il s'était imposé une moyenne quotidienne de douze bonnes actions qu'il portait à quinze ou seize quand son foie ou son estomac lui inspirait des inquiétudes.*   (S130)

He had set himself a daily average of twelve good deeds which he increased to fifteen or sixteen when anxieties over internal ailments inspired him.

Again the look back over one's shoulder. Then a final passé simple sentence closes the paragraph.

(104) *Une digestion un peu laborieuse de l'huissier valut ainsi une nouvelle augmentation de cinquante francs à Bourrichon qui, naguère encore, redoutait ce genre de malaise dont il faisait presque toujours les frais.* (S131)

A case of indigestion was thus worth a new raise of fifty francs to Bourrichon, who previously had always dreaded his employer's discomforts, which usually cost him dearly.

What is interesting here is that much of the important information of this paragraph, which I would entitle 'Amassing Good Deeds', is encoded in the plus-que-parfait. The important points would seem to be (1) that Malicorne did and recorded twelve good deeds on the first day, and (2) that he set a quota of twelve good deeds a day, which he sometimes exceeded. The first passé simple sentence (S129) may be seen as summing up Malicorne's activities, although it refers to his distributions to individual families rather than to the whole of his good deeds. The second passé simple (S131), however, seems to stand more as an example of the type of excess Malicorne was prone to when ill; thus it would relate to information in the subordinate clause of the sentence before.

The second paragraph (S132–135) seems to be more normal: a typical narrative paragraph encoding sequential events. It opens with an imparfait sentence that connects it with the previous paragraph.

(105) *Tant de bienfaits ne pouvaient passer inaperçus.* (S132)

So many good deeds could not pass unnoticed.

This implies an event: Malicorne's good deeds were noticed. Then there are several events, all in a chronological sequence: The rumor ran through the town that Malicorne was getting ready to run for office; Malicorne had a moment of discouragement; he got over it and redoubled his gifts; and he got the idea of extending his giving to a number of local charities.

This is a standard narrative paragraph; one that could be entitled 'Suspicion and Intensification of Effort'. The main points would be: (1) The townspeople refuse to believe in Malicorne, and (2) Malicorne redoubles his efforts. Two imparfait clauses serve as background: the first, a negative sentence, provides setting, and the second presents a background detail which is also a state.

The third paragraph (S136–140) has a different structure altogether. It could be entitled 'Success', and it can perhaps be summed up in the second

half of the first sentence, 'his reputation was [IMP] well established'.
Malicorne has had a breakthrough, and his fellow citizens now believe in
him. This sentence is expounded by another with two clauses, one in the
imparfait and one in the passé simple.

(106) *On le donnait* [IMP] *dans toute la ville comme un modèle de
    charité, et son exemple fut* [PS] *si entraînant que les dons se
    mirent à affluer de toutes parts aux entreprises philanthropiques...*
                                                              (S137)

The whole town considered [IMP] him to be a model of kindness, and his example was [PS] so irresistible that donations
started to flow in from all directions to philanthropic concerns...

This paragraph demonstrates clearly that we have moved into a different
type of discourse. Sentence 137 is the only one containing a passé simple.
In a different context, we might interpret the relationship of the first clause
of this sentence to the second in terms of background-event; however, in
the context of this paragraph, the true relation seems to be that of
thesis-result. Sentences 138–140, all in the imparfait, continue to develop
the theme in terms of generalities rather than in terms of sequenced
events. The event presented in the passé simple is not a focal one but
rather an incidental detail that is given as an example of a general state
depicted in the imparfait. In fact, this sentence represents an embedded
narrative: a sequence of events that was triggered by Malicorne's
generosity. This narrative, however, is contained in a subordinate clause,
and is backgrounded within the paragraph. Thus, the relationship of the
imparfait to the passé simple in this paragraph seems to be one of general
to specific: the imparfait is being used to give general characteristics, and
the passé simple is being used to give specific examples. The imparfait is
foreground, and the passé simple is background.
   This change of function on the part of the passé simple coincides with
the use of another plus-que-parfait form (in S136). This one, a passé
antérieur form, is a different kind of plus-que-parfait from the two we
examined earlier (S128 and S130), but the viewpoint is the same: one of
summing up the action from a forward vantage point. This plus-que-parfait, like the one found in S128, is introduced by an adverbial of time.
   What seems to have happened in these paragraphs is that the plus-que-
parfait has taken on the cohesive function of the passé simple. Up until
now, time reference in the text has always been paired with the passé
simple; however, now that the passé simple has assumed a different
function in relation to the imparfait, it cannot perform its normal role of

temporal succession. Thus, this function seems to have fallen to the plus-que-parfait forms, which are accordingly paired with time references. These plus-que-parfait constructions therefore chop off sections of time at their termination points rather than their beginning points, and the state of affairs previous to and coinciding with these termination points is then characterized by the imparfait. Thus, the introductory sentence S136:

(107) *En quatre mois, il eut dépensé ainsi près d'un dixième de sa fortune...* (S136)

In four months, he had spent in this way close to a tenth of his fortune...

The fourth paragraph (S141–146) appears to be another narrative paragraph that could be entitled 'Success II'. The thesis sentence sets a theme of 'Malicorne resting on his laurels':

(108) *Malicorne n'eut plus qu'à entretenir cette réputation et, tout en persévérant dans ses bonnes oeuvres, attendit d'un coeur tranquille que Dieu voulût bien le rappeler à lui.* (S141)

Malicorne had nothing more to do than to maintain this reputation and, while persevering in his good works, [he] waited with a tranquil heart for God to recall him to Himself.

The general-specific opposition of the third paragraph is now reversed; the two imparfait sentences beginning paragraph four give a habitual occurrence, a sort of recurring episode that illustrates Malicorne's high reputation in the town.

The fifth paragraph (S147–152) presents an exception to this general high opinion of Malicorne: Malicorne's wife. The theme of this paragraph might be 'No success at home', or perhaps, 'Side effects of success'. The central elements are her disapproval and Malicorne's guilty feelings. A result of this conflict is given in the passé simple (S151): Malicorne attempts to placate her with a money gift but she rejects his offer. This paragraph is somewhat difficult to categorize as it has a resolution of sorts and might be seen as a narrative paragraph with a long setting. It seems, however, that state is the more prominent element in this paragraph, with Malicorne's offer and his wife's refusal ranking as an incidental result of the overall state of affairs being described. This analysis is supported by the isolation of this passé simple clause: it cannot be said to necessarily succeed or to relate in any other way to sentence 141; it stands alone.

The sixth paragraph (S153–156) begins with another plus-que-parfait. It has become clear that the plus-que-parfait in this passage is also the 'bookkeeping line', giving us the current figures on Malicorne's good deeds and the amount of capital investment they represent. The plus-que-parfait is also paired with a time reference, i.e., S153 'at the end of a year'. This more or less specific point in time is then characterized by a number of imparfait constructions, which compose the main part of this paragraph.

In summary, episode 2a has two parts: six vignettes and six paragraphs. Although the six vignettes, which compose the narrow time margin portion, are clearly narrative, the following two paragraphs of widening time margin seem to constitute a transition into something that is more nearly a eulogy than a narrative. Paragraphs 3 (S136–140) and 6 (S153–156) are clear examples of this form.

Within these two paragraphs, the passé simple is no longer indicating sequential events nor providing any kind of cohesion to the section. Instead, it has become subsidiary to the imparfait, which is the predominant tense. Thus, contingent temporal succession no longer characterizes these paragraphs. Instead, they are connected to the storyline of the text by occasional plus-que-parfait constructions, which thus constitute a simple chronological backbone.

These paragraph structures must be considered to be [−contingent] temporal succession. They do, however, exhibit agent orientation. The parameters of [−contingent] succession and [+agent] orientation would indicate some type of behavioral discourse; thus this category appears to fit. Longacre characterizes behavioral, eulogy-type discourse as using a customary past tense, and the imparfait forms in this section do have customary or habitual meaning.

6.6. Episode 2b1. This episode consists of three long paragraphs (S157–159, 160–170, and 171–176) and the majority of a fourth paragraph (S177–185).

As we noted earlier, this section begins with an introductory clause that gives the time and the location as well as other details of setting. The time adverbial, 'one morning', sets the time margin as narrow and specific. This first sentence (S157) also has a passé simple verb form, thus the specificity of time is paired with boundedness of tense. The predicate used is 'feel troubled', one which we might normally expect to see more often in the imparfait than in the passé simple. In the passé simple, it might have a meaning of either momentariness or inception. The second sentence, however, makes the proper meaning clear:

(109) *C'était une espèce d'incertitude poignante et mélancholique ne se rapportant à aucun objet précis et qu'il ne lui souvenait pas d'avoir jamais éprouvée.*   (S158)

It was a kind of sharp and melancholic uncertainty that didn't seem related to any particular object and that he didn't remember ever having experienced before.

This feeling was not limited to a single moment, so the meaning must be one of inception. Furthermore, this inceptive boundary set by the passé simple is making a clear division between this moment (when the feeling began) and all past time (in which such a feeling had never occurred).

The second sentence (S158), an equative imparfait construction, describes the concept introduced in the first. It represents a state and must be considered background material.

The third sentence (S159) is a plus-que-parfait construction, introduced by the conjunction 'however'. By virtue of this conjunction, the sentence stands in opposition to the thesis introduced in the first sentence.

The first paragraph thus has a thesis sentence in the passé simple and the next two sentences explore that thesis, almost as if they represented Malicorne's thoughts about it. The relationship might be described as thesis, amplification, and antithesis. The passé simple construction, as a thesis sentence linked with a punctiliar time adverbial, is clearly the foreground here.

The second paragraph (S160–170) is much longer and seems to carry the following information: Malicorne enters a building, one that is well-known to him, and goes up to the third floor [PS]. / The building is old, dark, and dilapidated [IMP]. This building is no different from any other that Malicorne has seen [IMP]. However, his feeling of anxiety has become more piercing [PQP], and it seems about to be explained [IMP]. / Malicorne hears a child cry and knocks on an apartment door [PS].

At first glance, this appears to be a narrative paragraph, one in a chain that is moving the character to a particular place and thus is advancing the storyline. However, we have to consider not only the overall structure of this episode but also the internal structure of this paragraph. In terms of this structure, the actions of Malicorne are almost marginal, representing opening and closure. The nucleus of the paragraph appears to be the description of the house and its relation to Malicorne's feelings.

In summary, several sentences of description of a building are reduced to one proposition: 'The building is old, dark, and dilapidated'. This is followed by a comparison or evaluation statement, relating the building to Malicorne's experience as a bailiff. Finally, there is an opposition or contrast statement describing the effect on Malicorne's peculiar feeling.

Almost all of this nuclear portion is encoded in the imparfait. The one exception is the clause that introduces Malicorne's feeling; this is another plus-que-parfait construction introduced by 'however'. Malicorne's feeling was thematic in the last paragraph and it is no less so in this one. This paragraph might be entitled 'The Tenement Building and Malicorne's Peculiar Feeling' to reflect these two thematic elements. In terms of the structure of the paragraph itself, therefore, the imparfait rather than the passé simple seems to be the foreground or mainline tense.

The third paragraph (S171–176) contains even less narration. The title of this paragraph might be 'The Apartment and Malicorne's Peculiar Feeling'. The information given in mainline clauses is roughly this: The apartment consisted of only two narrow rooms, and the first was even darker than the hall [IMP]. / A thin, tired-looking young woman greeted Malicorne [PS]. / A small child was holding onto her skirt [IMP]. The second room contained a simple bed, a small table, two chairs, and an old sewing machine [IMP]. The poverty of this apartment was nothing that Malicorne had not seen before [IMP], but for the first time in his life, Malicorne was feeling intimidated in a poor person's house [IMP].

Again, there is a linkage to the main story: the one passé simple sentence. Within the paragraph as a unit, however, this linking sentence is clearly subordinated, even at the risk of clarity. The description of the apartment begins before it has even been stated that Malicorne has been let into the apartment. The opening of the door and Malicorne's entrance must be inferred from the first two sentences:

(110) *Le logement était de deux pièces.... Une femme mince...*
accueillit Malicorne. (S171, 172)

The apartment consisted of two rooms... A slender woman... greeted Malicorne.

The first sentence introduces the thematic element, the apartment, and the second, almost as an interruption, depicts a speech act-event.

The nucleus of this paragraph is the description followed by some sort of author evaluation and contrast in yet another opposition frame: The apartment is small, dark, and bare. This should not trouble Malicorne; but, Malicorne is feeling troubled.

The importance of this last reflection is underlined by an adverbial introducer in S176 'for the first time in his life'. This sentence represents the culmination of the paragraph, and it is in the imparfait. Thus the imparfait appears again to be the mainline or foreground tense of a paragraph.

(111) *Mais pour la première fois de sa vie, Malicorne se sentait*
intimidé en entrant chez un pauvre. (S176)

But for the first time in his life, Malicorne was feeling intimidated in entering the house of a poor person.

The fourth paragraph (S176–187) begins with an evaluation-opposition frame, the most extended yet:

(112) *Habituellement, ses visites de charité **étaient** des plus brèves. Sans s'asseoir, il **posait** quelques questions précises, **débitait** une formule d'encouragement et, lâchant son aumône, **prenait** aussitôt la porte. Cette fois, il ne **savait** plus très bien pourquoi il était venu et ne **pensait** plus à mettre la main à son portefeuille. Les idées **tremblaient** dans sa tête et les paroles sur ses lèvres. Il **osait** à peine lever les yeux sur la petite couturière en songeant à sa profession d'huissier.* (S177–181)

Habitually, his charity visits **were** very brief. Without sitting down, he **would ask** several specific questions, **utter** an encourging phrase, and, dropping his alm, **would** immediately **head for** the door. **This time**, he no longer **knew** very well why he had come and he didn't **think** to reach for his billfold. Ideas **trembled** in his head and words on his lips. He hardly **dared** lift his eyes to the little seamstress in thinking of his profession of bailiff.

The theme of this paragraph has obviously been set as 'The Visit'. First it offers a contrast between Malicorne's usual behavior during a charity visit and his behavior at this point. It goes on to describe the woman's behavior and to narrate that of the child. Finally, there is an interruption that puts an end to the interaction (and opens the next episode).

The opening sentences of this paragraph are interesting because we have a habitual passage and a state in juxtaposition. Three of the imparfait forms in the habitual passage are nonstate verbs; however, the 'state of affairs' that they present is conjoined with the following description of Malicorne's emotional state. This passage seems to equate the two, saying 'this was the state before and this is the state now'. The paragraph is divided in terms of the dominant tense, with a series of nine imparfait forms followed by seven passé simples. The first part of the paragraph offers the final and most extensive opposition frame, a sort of culmination of the series. The first five passé simple forms that follow seem to add details of the visit. The last two belong to the next episode.

Thus, at a paragraph level, the imparfait constructions in this episode appear to represent foreground rather than background. However, rather than events, they present true states or, in the habitual mode, states of affairs.

How should this section be analyzed? We can certainly characterize the passé simple as representing chronological temporal succession overall within the episode; however, at a paragraph level, the passé simple constructions seem to be subordinated to the status of a margin, or even an interruption. They are also less prominent within this episode as a whole, encoding only internal events (sudden or intense emotions) and participant movement. The imparfait, on the other hand, has become the tense of the paragraph nucleus, which can best be characterized in terms of comparison/contrast frames.

Two notions from Longacre prove helpful at this point. The first is the classification of discourse types introduced in (78) at the beginning of this chapter. It is essential to determine whether these paragraphs belong to the category of narrative or whether they represent a different type of discourse. In fact, they do not adhere to the criteria for narrative in the classification. We have seen that each of these paragraphs are organized around some type of theme: "The Building," "The Apartment," or "The Visit," which it characterizes and then relate to another theme. Even the first sentence, which begins with a passé simple construction, is built around a theme of "Malicorne's Peculiar Feeling." They seem thus to be more theme oriented than participant oriented and would be [−agent] orientation.

Since the paragraph nuclei consist only of descriptions and comparison/contrast frames, it seems that these paragraphs would also be [−contingent] temporal succession. However, their value in relation to this parameter is more difficult to determine. There is a definite progression from one comparison frame to the next, which is mostly manifested in the intensification of Malicorne's peculiar feeling and the expansion of the comparison/contrast frame.

Despite this difficulty, these paragraphs resemble expository discourse more than any other of the four types. Longacre (1983:8) characterizes expository discourse as "quite distinct in its preference for existential and equational clauses—often with considerable nominalization." These types of constructions are very noticeable in this section. He further characterizes expository discourse as oriented towards themes rather than participants, and this description also fits this section. We will thus consider 2b2 to be expository rather than narrative.

The second helpful concept from Longacre is that of discourse PEAK. This term is defined as "any episode-like unit set apart by special surface structure features and corresponding to the Climax or Denouement in the notional structure" (Longacre 1983:24).

Longacre has described a number of devices that an author can use to mark a peak. Among these techniques, which he calls the author's "bag of tricks," are such phenomena as rhetorical underlining (to slow down the pace of the action), a shift in surface structure tense, variation in the size of constructions, and a shift from monologue to dialogue or from dialogue to drama (Longacre 1981:25–38). Due to the disturbance of so many norms of narrative at peak, Longacre (1983:25) characterizes peak as a "zone of turbulence" within a narrative.

In this episode, we have already observed a number of oddities: the shift to imparfait as the foreground tense at the paragraph level, the long paragraphs, and the comparison/contrast frames. All of these are common markings of peak zones. The comparison/contrast frames, with their constant reiteration of one or two concepts, can be identified as a type of rhetorical underlining. This section then can be seen to constitute a peak zone preceding the climax of the narrative. We will discuss the relevance of peak further in §§6.9–11.

6.7. Episode 2b2. The quiet serenity of "The Visit" is suddenly interrupted by a jolting event: there is a loud, violent rapping at the door. From this point on, the paragraphs are short and simple. Speech acts dominate, but dynamic actions are also prominent. There is, however, one last comparison paragraph, consisting of one sentence with a verb in the plus-que-parfait of the subjunctive and one sentence with a verb in the imparfait. This seems to be another intrusion of the author, making a comparison between a hypothetical emotional response in the past and Malicorne's state of emotions now.

(113) *Dans un autre temps, Malicorne eût admiré en connaisseur l'entrain avec lequel Gorgerin menait la rude besogne qui consiste à encaisser les loyers des pauvres. Mais il éprouvait le même sentiment de crainte qui faisait battre le coeur de l'enfant réfugié dans ses bras.* (S200–201)

In another time, Malicorne would have admired as a connoisseur the spirit with which Gorgerin conducted the rough job of collecting rent from the poor. But he **was feeling** the same fear that was making the child's heart pound [for the child had taken refuge in his arms].

There are three other imparfait forms used in this section. All contain material that is nonmainline or background. One, (S202), is a quote formula, showing that the speech act (of Gorgerin's) that it presents was repeated several times. This imparfait creates a backdrop for an action of Malicorne's in the following sentence (S204). The next imparfait also has Gorgerin as its subject. It is of the same type as sentences 65 and 74 in episode 1:

(114) *Interloqué, Gorgerin le considérait avec des yeux stupides.* (S208)

Speechless, Gorgerin stared at him stupidly.

Finally there is another author intrusion, used as a response to a comment of Gorgerin's.

(115) *Effectivement, Malicorne perdait la tête...* (S212)

As a matter of fact, Malicorne was losing his mind...

This clause is referring both to the unusual action that Malicorne has already committed—ordering the owner of the building out of the apartment and to his attack on Gorgerin. This then is another instance where the nonboundedness of the imparfait appears to be its defining characteristic.

As in episodes 1 and 3, the passé simple constructions represent sequential events which correspond to the foreground. The imparfait constructions present either states or states of affairs and thus constitute the background.

6.8. Surface structure findings. What discourse functions might the passé simple and the imparfait perform in a behavioral discourse? The function that emerged from our analysis of these paragraphs was a general-specific opposition, in which the imparfait forms characterized a state and isolated passé simple forms gave specific events as examples. This function would designate the imparfait as foreground or mainline and the passé simple as background, and thus represent a reversal of the narrative foregrounding/backgrounding relation. However, a definition of the imparfait as state and the passé simple as event would provide a link between two such opposing functions.

We have thus discovered at least three different discourse types within this narrative text: narrative discourse, some type of expository (descriptive) discourse, and some type of behavioral discourse. In each of these, the passé simple/imparfait opposition had different characteristics.

At the beginning of this chapter, a claim by Weinrich that the passé simple/imparfait opposition represented the only function of these tenses in the narrated world was presented. How would our findings be accounted for within Weinrich's theory?

Weinrich's narrated world is characterized by the use of the imparfait, the passé simple, the plus-que-parfait, the passé antérieur, and the conditional tenses among others. His "commented world," on the other hand, is characterized by the use of the present tense, the passé composé, and the future.

All the tenses of "L'huissier," except for those used in spoken dialogue, would fall into the first category. Thus all three of our discourse types would also be classified in Weinrich's narrated world. Weinrich's claim, therefore, as well as his discourse typology, does not hold.

On the other hand, we have the claim that the passé simple and the imparfait have meanings that underlie their discourse functions. In the case of the passé simple, this meaning is event, defined in terms of boundedness, and, in the case of the imparfait, this meaning is state, defined in terms of nonboundedness. It was further claimed that these meanings could account for all the occurrences of the passé simple and the imparfait in a discourse.

In this section, it has been shown through a constituent analysis of the text that the passé simple forms encode bounded events and the imparfait forms encode nonbounded states. It was demonstrated that, in the narrative sections of this discourse, the function of the passé simple can be defined as foregrounding and that of the imparfait as backgrounding, and that these functions are thus correlated with the concepts of event and state. The passé simple and the imparfait may occur in other discourse types (in expository and behavioral, specifically), and they may have functions within these which differ from their narrative functions. However, these different functions are explained in terms of the basic concepts of state and event.

6.9–6.11 Notional structure of "L'huissier"

Surface structure features in a text can be assumed to correspond to a deeper level notional structure motivating that text (Longacre 1983). For this text, the six-section constituent structure seems to correspond to the following general plot or notional structure for narrative (Longacre 1981:337):[13]

---

[13]It should be noted that this notional structure is not in one-to-one correspondence with the surface structure. The distinction between the two is that the notional structure represents the individual components of episode 2 as occupying the same level as the stage, episode 1, and episode 3. Although this represents a departure from Longacre's model, such a notional structure is appropriate for this text. Episode 2 seems to me a difficult section to categorize because it contains both peak and nonpeak elements. Longacre has noted that the peak (notional structure CLIMAX) of an embedded peak discourse marks the peak (or highest point of tension) for the entire text, "just as Akron is the highest point in Summit County which is in turn the highest county in Ohio" (Longacre 1983:34). Episodes 2b1 and 2b2, which both carry peak markings, do represent the highest point of tension for the text as a whole. On the other hand, episode 2a, which redefines the character of Malicorne, is taken to be the low point of tension for "L'huissier" as a whole. Episode 2 is considered to constitute three components of the overall notional structure: RESTAGING (author's term), MOUNTING TENSION, and CLIMAX.

(116) Surface slot   Sentences   Function   Section

Surface slot	Sentences	Function	Section
Stage	1	EXPOSITION	1
Episode 1	2–80	INCITING INCIDENT	2
Episode 2a	81–156	RESTAGING	3
Episode 2b1	157–185	MOUNTING TENSION	4
Episode 2b2	186–216	CLIMAX	5
Episode 3	217–233	DENOUEMENT	6

From this point on, I use either section numbers (1–6) or notional structure functions (INCITING INCIDENT, MOUNTING TENSION, etc.) to refer to different parts of the text.

6.9. Tension level and peak markings. As noted earlier, the CLIMAX is often the easiest notional structure constituent to identify in a narrative text due to special markings of the "peak" (Longacre 1983:25). The CLIMAX may be described as a point of high emotional intensity for the reader.

In §6.5 concerning episode 2a, we looked at a number of devices that an author can use to mark a peak. Several of these techniques intersect in MOUNTING TENSION.

Perhaps the most important peak marker in this text is rhetorical underlining. The form it takes here is a series of two or three proposition comparison/contrast frames that occur closer and closer together until they culminate in a six-sentence comparison just before the beginning of the CLIMAX. The underlined point can be summarized as "Today is different from all the other days of Malicorne's life, although there is no apparent reason that it should be." These comparison frames involve sentences 158–160, 168–169, 175–176, and 177–181 of the MOUNTING TENSION. Only one such comparison frame is found in the CLIMAX (S200–201) and none appear anywhere outside these two sections.

Other important markings on MOUNTING TENSION include its use of the imparfait for the foreground, long paragraphs, and a greater amount of nominalization.

The CLIMAX has only one comparison frame but possesses other markings of peak. Perhaps the most important marking on this section is its large proportion of vivid dialogue. This is significant because there are only two dialogue parts within all of episode 2 (RESTAGING, MOUNTING TENSION, and CLIMAX SECTIONS).

The peak of this discourse thus seems to correspond to the sections of MOUNTING TENSION and CLIMAX (S157–216).

The climactic moment of the story occurs during the confrontation between the protagonist Malicorne and the antagonist Gorgerin at the moment where the verbal conflict turns physical. Malicorne initiates the attack, but is then killed by Gorgerin. The entire fight takes only two sentences.

One reason that it only takes two sentences is that the speech act which accompanies Malicorne's attack is introduced in the same sentence as the attack. It is subordinated to the main verb in the following way:

(117) *[Malicorne]* **se rua** [PS] *sur Gorgerin et* **le jeta** [PS] *hors du logis* **en vociférant:** *«Un sale cochon de propriétaire, oui. A bas les propriétaires! A bas les propriétaires!»* (S212–215)

[Malicorne] **flung himself** [PS] at Gorgerin and **threw him** [PS] out of the apartment, **yelling:** "A filthy swine of a landlord, yes. Down with landlords! Down with landlords!"

This combining of an action with a speech act seems to add a greater sense of importance or vividness to the proposition. We find it also at a pivotal moment in the embedded INCITING INCIDENT narrative when an infuriated Saint Peter sentences Malicorne to Hell:

(118) *Tant de paisible cynisme indigna* [PS] *Saint Pierre qui s'écria en se tournant vers les anges: «En Enfer!»* (S25–26)

So much peaceful cynicism infuriated [PS] Saint Peter **who cried out as he turned to the angels:** "Into Hell!"

In both of these examples, the quote formula is subordinated as a participle or relative clause and tacked onto a strong action proposition, apparently to condense the action and thus increase the level of tension. It is a mild example perhaps of the "packing of the eventline" that is commonly used to signal action peaks (Longacre 1981:349).

Peak characteristics can thus be seen in three sections of our text: MOUNTING TENSION, CLIMAX, and INCITING INCIDENT. The peak in the INCITING INCIDENT seems, however, to mark a peak only for that section, which is an embedded narrative discourse with its own setting, climax, and denouement. The peak which occurs in the CLIMAX, on the other hand, seems to mark the point of maximum tension for the whole text.

6.10. Stage or setting and climactic sections. Some sections of this text thus encode climactic events while others do not. These nonclimactic sections seem to provide information and context for the events that follow. The EXPOSITION, for example, is a one-sentence stage, performing the function of exposition for the INCITING INCIDENT. It is a very short exposition, partly because further exposition is provided elsewhere in the text. The INCITING INCIDENT begins with a dramatic event: the death of the protagonist, Malicorne. Next, there is his judgment before Saint Peter, a judgment in which he is speedily sentenced to hell. Angels then swoop down to carry him off. An appeal is made to a higher authority, God, and He and Saint Peter disagree. Saint Peter is overruled, and Malicorne escapes hell to return to earth. Thus the tension level starts high and continues high in this section.

The MOUNTING TENSION builds up the tension slowly from a fairly low level to the highpoint of the CLIMAX. As we have seen, MOUNTING TENSION and CLIMAX form two parts of what is really one episode. The MOUNTING TENSION, which contains long descriptions of participants and of physical surroundings seems to set up an elaborate stage for the two climactic events which occur in the CLIMAX, namely, Malicorne's defense of the poor woman against his friend Gorgerin and then Malicorne's death at the hand of Gorgerin. The majority of the actions recounted in the MOUNTING TENSION involve motion, moving the participants into position for the CLIMAX.

The RESTAGING is more difficult to categorize, but it seems to be a type of resetting or restaging that bridges the gap between the INCITING INCIDENT and the MOUNTING TENSION and CLIMAX. In this way it serves as a setting for the entire episode recounted in the MOUNTING TENSION and CLIMAX and also for the final episode, the DENOUEMENT in which Malicorne finally achieves his goal of acceptance into Heaven. Earlier, we distinguished two types of setting for Gorgerin's visit, a general setting, i.e., Gorgerin was a landowner who often came to Malicorne when tenants could not pay, and the specific setting, i.e., **this time**, he was coming to see Malicorne about a family who was two terms behind on their rent. Thus, the setting for the events in the CLIMAX seems to me to have two parts: (1) the general setting or state of affairs—Malicorne was a man respected by his community for his acts of charity, which is presented in the RESTAGING, and (2) the specific setting—this charity visit was taking place in this particular building and the family involved was like this and **this time**, Malicorne was behaving in this particular way (presented in the MOUNTING TENSION). Indeed, **this time** seems to be a key concept all throughout that section.

An earlier chart of verb forms for the four part constituent structure showed that episode 2 as a whole had a much larger proportion of imparfait forms than either episode 1 or episode 3. Later we saw that these imparfait forms were concentrated in the first and second sections of episode 2 (RESTAGING and MOUNTING TENSION). If we now look at a tally of verb forms for all six notional structure sections together with the distinctions that we have just made between "setting" sections and "climactic event" sections, we can see some interesting correspondences.

(119) Correlation of verb distribution and notional structure sections

Section	Passé simple	Imparfait	Other	
1	1	2	1	Setting
2	25	4	2	
3	34	32	5	Setting
4	13	23	4	Setting
5	15	5	1	
6	9	1	0	

The sections that serve as "settings" for other sections are correlated with a high occurrence of imparfait forms, the majority of which encode true states or cluster as state of affairs paragraphs. In the sections that contain "climactic events," mostly events involving transition between heaven and earth, the passé simple forms seem to outnumber imparfaits by a ratio of 3 to 1 or higher.

6.11. Summary of notional structure. We have found that there is correlation between the proportions of passé simple and imparfait forms found within each section and the function that that section serves. The INCITING INCIDENT, CLIMAX, and DENOUEMENT sections, which have passé simple to imparfait ratios of 6 to 1, 3 to 1, and 9 to 1, respectively, correspond to climactic event passages in the narrative. The RESTAGING and MOUNTING TENSION sections, in which the number of imparfait forms is roughly equivalent to or greater than the number of passé simple forms, correspond to setting for the other sections.

6.12. Summary. In this chapter, it was demonstrated that the concept of event, defined in terms of boundedness, and the concept of state, defined in terms of nonboundedness, can account for all of the occurrences of the passé simple and the imparfait in a discourse. These basic meanings of the two tenses underlie a foregrounding/backgrounding function of the passé simple/imparfait opposition in narrative discourse as well as different functions of the two tenses in the other types of discourse found in the text, "L'huissier."

6.13. Conclusions. Conclusions arrived at from this study are summarized as follows:

1. Many varied definitions have been put forth to explain the use of the imparfait, most of which appear to have little in common. There is one feature, nonboundedness, which can be considered a core value of the imparfait, in that it ties together many of the qualities which have been recognized as characterizing the imparfait. By equating the imparfait with nonboundedness and the passé simple with boundedness, a number of approaches to the passé simple/imparfait opposition can be explained.

2. A bounded predication can be identified with the concept of event and a nonbounded predication with the concept of state. In the analysis of communication, an event is what is seen as an event by the speaker and a state is what is seen as a state by the speaker.

3. The relationship between verb or predicate types and the passé simple and imparfait is complex. As we have seen in chapter three, there is a tendency for verbs that have an inherent feature of boundedness (i.e., telic verbs) to occur in the passé simple and for verbs that are inherently nonbounded (i.e., atelic verbs) to occur in the imparfait. However, telic verbs or predicates may occur in the imparfait and atelic verbs or predicates in the passé simple; such uses result in a modification of the meaning of the verb or predicate. There are also other categories of verbs which do not appear to have an inherent value for boundedness but possess both bounded and nonbounded senses.

4. The imparfait can be seen to represent nonboundedness and a subjective view of state in the many different uses of the imparfait which have been distinguished by French grammarians. The passé simple can be seen to represent boundedness and a subjective view of event, even in its use with stative verbs.

5. The imparfait can be seen to represent state and the passé simple can be seen to represent event in all their uses within a French narrative discourse. Within narrative discourse, event and state correlate with the functions of foregrounding and backgrounding. In other types of discourse, the passé simple and the imparfait may have different functions. However, the basic values of event and state will inform all functions assigned to the passé simple and the imparfait.

Appendix

Glossed Text of "L'huissier" by Marcel Aymé

"L'huissier"[14]

(S1) *Il*   *y*   *avait,*   *dans une petite ville de France,*
     <dummy^subject> there have^IMP^3s in   a   small city of France

     un huissier qui s'appelait   *Malicorne et*   *il*   *était*   *si*
     a   bailiff   who himself^call^IMP^3s Malicorne and he be^IMP^3s so

     scrupuleux dans l'accomplissement   *de son triste ministère qu'il*
     scrupulous in   the^accomplishment of his   sad   ministry that^he

     n'eût   *pas hésité*   *à saisir*   *ses propres*
     NEG^have^IMPSBJ^3s NEG hesitate^PSTPCPL to seize^INF his own

     meubles, mais l'occasion   *ne*   *s'en*   *présenta*   *pas et,*
     furniture but   the^occasion NEG itself^of^it present^PS^3s NEG and

     du   *reste, il paraît*   *que la loi ne*   *permet*   *pas à*
     of^the rest   it appear^PRES^3s that the law NEG permit^PRES^3s NEG to

     un huissier d'instrumenter   *contre lui-même.*
     a   bailiff   to^take^action^INF against him-self

     There once was, in a small city of France, a bailiff named Malicorne, who was
     so scrupulous in the accomplishment of his sad duties that he wouldn't have
     hesitated to seize his own furniture, but the occason never arose and, in any
     case, it appears that the law doesn't allow a bailiff to take action against
     himself.

(S2) *Une nuit qu'il*   *reposait*   *auprès de sa femme, Malicorne mourut*
     One night that^he rest^PS^3s near   to his wife   Malicorne die^PS^3s

     en dormant   *et fut*   *aussitôt admis*   *à Pierre,*
     in sleep^PRSPCPL and be^PS^3s as^soon admit^PSTPCPL to Peter

     comparaître   *devant*   *saint Pierre qui juge*   *en*
     appear^in^court^INF in^front^of saint Peter who judge^PRES^3s in

     première instance.
     first   hearing

     One night as he was lying next to his wife, Malicorne died in his sleep and
     was immediately admitted to appear before Saint Peter, who is responsible for
     the first judgment.

(S3) *Le grand saint Porte-Clés l'accueillit*   *froidement.*
     the great saint carry-keys him^greet^PS^3s coldly

     The great saint Gatekeeper greeted him coldly.

---

[14]"L'huissier" by Marcel Aymé. Le passe-muraille. EDITIONS GALLIMARD. Used by
permission.

(S4)   —*Vous vous   appelez   Malicorne et   vous êtes   huissier.*
       you   yourself call^PRES^2 Malicorne and you be^PRES^2 bailiff

       "Your name is Malicorne and you are a bailiff.

(S5)   *Il   n'y   en   a   guère au*
       < dummy^subject > NEG^there of^them have^PRES^3s hardly in^the

       Paradis.
       paradise

       There are hardly any of those in Heaven."

(S6)   —*Ça ne   fait   rien,   répondit   Malicorne.*
       that NEG make^PRES^3s nothing answer^PS^3s Malicorne

       "That doesn't matter," answered Malicorne.

(S7)   *Je ne   tiens   pas autrement à être   avec des   confrères.*
       I   NEG hold^PRES^1s NEG otherwise to be^INF with PART^the colleagues

       "I don't particularly care about being with my colleagues, anyway."

(S8)   *Tout en surveillant   la   mise   en   place d'une immense*
       all in supervise^PRSPCPL the put^PSTPCPL into place of^an immense

       cuve, apparemment remplie   d'eau,   qu'une troupe d'anges
       vat   apparently   fill^PSTPCPL with^water that^a troop of^angels

       venait   d'apporter,   saint Pierre eut   un sourire d'ironie.
       come^IMP^3s to^bring^INF saint Peter have^PS^3s a smile   of^irony

       As he supervised the placement of an immense vat, apparently filled with
       water, that a troop of angels had just brought, Saint Peter smiled ironically.

(S9)   —*Il me   semble,   mon garçon, que vous avez   pas mal*
       it to^me seem^PRES^3s my boy   that you have^PRES^2 NEG badly

       d'illusions.
       of^illusions

       "It seems to me, my boy, that you have many illusions."

(S10) —*J'espère,   dit   Malicorne, voilà   tout.*
       I^hope^PRES^1s say^PS^3s Malicorne that^is all

       "I have hopes," said Malicorne, "that's all.

(S11) *D'ailleurs, je me   sens   la   conscience plutôt tranquille.*
       besides   I myself feel^PRES^1s the conscience rather tranquil

       Besides, I feel that my conscience is pretty clear.

(S12) *Bien entendu,   je suis   un abominable pécheur, un vase*
       well understand^PSTPCPL I be^PRES^1s an abominable sinner   a vase

d'iniquités,   une vermine impure.
of^iniquities a   vermin impure

Of course, I am an abominable sinner, a vessel filled with iniquity, an unclean vermin.

(S13) *Ceci dit,   il reste   que je n'ai   jamais*
this say^PS^3s it remain^PRES^3s that I NEG^have^PRES^1s never

fait   tort   d'un sou   à personne, que j'allais
do^PSTPCPL wrong in^a penny to no^one   that I^go^IMP^1s

régulièrement à la   messe et   que je m'acquittais   des
regularly   to the mass and that I myself^acquit^IMP^1s of^the

devoirs de ma charge d'huissier à la   satisfaction générale.
duties of my charge of^bailiff to the satisfaction general

Having said that, it remains that I've never cheated anyone of a penny, that I attended mass regularly and that I've fulfilled the duties of my office of bailiff to the general satisfaction."

(S14) *—Vraiment? fit   saint Pierre.*
truly   say^PS^3s saint Peter

"Really?," said Saint Peter.

(S15) *Regardez   donc cette grande cuve qui vient   de monter*
look^at^PRES^2 then this great   vat that come^PRES^3s to ascend^INF

au   ciel avec votre dernier soupir.
to^the sky with your last   breath.

"Then look at that big vat that just ascended to heaven with your last breath.

(S16) *Que croyez-vous   qu'elle contienne?*
what believe^PRES^2-you that^it contain^PRSSBJ^3s

What do you think it contains?"

(S17) *—Je n'en   ai   pas la   moindre idée.*
I   NEG^of^it have^PRES^1s NEG the least   idea

"I haven't the least idea."

(S18) *—Eh bien, elle est   pleine des   larmes de la   veuve et   de*
INTJ   well it be^PRES^3s full of^the tears of the widow and of

l'orphelin   que vous avez   réduits   au   désespoir.
the^orphan that you have^PRES^2 reduce^PSTPCPL to^the despair

"Well, it's full of the tears of the widow and the orphan that you have reduced to despair."

(S19) *L'huissier considéra   la   cuve et   son amer contenu et*
the^bailiff consider^PS^3s the vat   and its bitter contents and

repartit   sans   se   démonter:
reply^PS^3s without himself take^apart^INF

The bailiff considered the vat and its bitter contents and replied calmly:

(S20) *—C'est   bien possible.*
it^be^PRES^3s well possible

"That's very possible.

(S21) *Quand la veuve et   l'orphelin sont   des   mauvais*
when   the widow and the^orphan be^PRES^3p PART^the bad

payeurs, il faut   recourir à   la saisie mobilière.
payors   it be^necessary^PRES^3s resort^INF to the seizure furnishing

When the widow and the orphan are bad payers, you have to resort to the
seizure of their furniture.

(S22) *Ceci ne   va   pas sans   des   pleurs et   des*
this NEG go^PRES^3s NEG without PART^the tears and PART^the

grincements de dents, vous pensez   bien.
grindings   of teeth   you think^PRES^2 well

That doesn't happen without tears and the grinding of teeth, you know.

(S23) *Aussi n'est-il   pas surprenant   que la cuve*
also   NEG^be^PRES^3s-it NEG surprise^PRSPCPL that the vat

soit   pleine.
be^PRSSBJ^3s full

So it's not surprising that the vat should be full.

(S24) *Dieu merci, mes affaires marchaient bien et je n'ai   pas*
God thank my affairs   run^IMP^3p well and I NEG^have^PRES^1s NEG

chômé.
be^unemployed^PSTPCPL

Thank God, business was good and I've never been without work."

(S25) *Tant   de paisible   cynisme indigna   saint Pierre qui*
so^much of peace^able cynicism anger^PS^3s saint Peter who

s'écria   en se   tournant   vers   les anges:
himself^cry^out^PS^3s in himself turn^PRSPCPL toward the angels

So much peaceful cynicism infuriated Saint Peter who cried out as he turned
to the angels:

(S26)   —*En   enfer!*
        into   hell

        "Into hell!

(S27)   *Qu'on   me   l'accommode   d'un   bon   feu   et*
        that^one to^me   him^accommodate^PRES^3s   with^a good   fire and

        qu'on   m'entretienne   ses   brûlures pour l'éternité   en
        that^one for^me^maintain^PRSSBJ^3s   his   burns   for   the^eternity   in

        les   arrosant   deux fois par jour avec les larmes de la   veuve
        them   irrigate^PRSPCPL   two   time per   day   with the tears   of the widow

        et   de   l'orphelin!
        and   of   the^orphan

        Let him be set up with a roaring fire and let his burns be treated for eternity
        by soaking twice a day with the tears of the widow and the orphan."

(S28)   *Déjà   les   anges   se   précipitaient.*
        already the   angels themself   descend^IMP^3p

        Already the angels were descending.

(S29)   *Malicorne les   arrêta   d'un   geste   très   ferme.*
        Malicorne   them   stop^PS^3s with^a gesture very   firm

        Malicorne stopped them with a very firm gesture.

(S30)   —*Minute, dit-il.*
        minute   say^PRES^3s-he

        "Just a minute," said he.

(S31)   *J'en   appelle à Dieu de ce   jugement inique.*
        I^of^it   appeal to God   of this judgment unjust

        "I appeal this unjust judgment to God."

(S32)   *La procédure est   la   procédure.*
        the procedure be^PRES^3s   the procedure

        Procedure is procedure.

(S33)   *Saint Pierre, rageur, dut   suspendre   l'exécution   de*
        saint Peter   choleric be^obliged^to^PS^3s   suspend^INF   the^execution of

        sa   sentence.
        his sentence

        Saint Peter, furious, had to suspend the execution of his sentence.

(S34)   *Dieu ne   se   fit   pas   attendre   et, précédé*
        God   NEG   himself make^PS^3s   NEG   wait^for^INF   and precede^PSTPCPL

d'un   roulement de tonnerre, entra   sur un nuage.
by^a rolling   of thunder enter^PS^3s on a   cloud

God didn't waste any time in arriving; preceded by a rumbling of thunder, he entered on a cloud.

(S35) *Lui non plus   ne   paraissait   pas avoir   les huissiers en*
He NEG either NEG appear^IMP^3s NEG have^INF the bailiffs in

grande faveur.
great favor

He didn't seem to hold bailiffs in any great favor either.

(S36) *On le vit   bien à sa façon   bourrue d'interroger   Malicorne.*
one it see^PS^3s well in his manner rough   of^question^INF Malicorne

One could see that by the rough manner in which He questioned Malicorne.

(S37) —*Mon Dieu, répondit   celui-ci,   voilà   ce qui se*
my   God answer^PS^3s this^one-here there^is this that himself

passe.
pass^PRES^3s

"My God," Malicorne replied, "This is what is happening.

(S38) *Saint Pierre m'impute   les larmes de la   veuve et   de*
saint Peter to^me^impute^PRES^3s the tears   of the widow and of

l'orphelin   que j'ai   fait   couler   dans
the^orphan that I^have^PRES^1s make^PSTPCPL flow^INF in

l'exercice   de ma charge d'huissier, et   il dispose   que ces
the^exercise of my charge of^bailiff and he decide^PRES^3s that these

larmes brûlantes   seront   l'instrument   de mon supplice éternel.
tears   burn^PRSPCPL be^FUT^3p the^instrument of my   torment eternal

Saint Peter is holding me responsible for the tears of the widow and the orphan that I caused to flow in the performance of my duties as a bailiff, and he has decided that these scalding tears will be the instrument of my eternal torment.

(S39) *C'est   une injustice.*
this^be^PRES^3s an   injustice

This is an injustice."

(S40) —*Evidemment, dit   Dieu en se   tournant   vers   saint*
evidently   say^PS^3s God in himself turn^PRSPCPL toward saint

Pierre avec un front   sévère.
Peter with a forehead severe

"Obviously," said God, turning to Saint Peter with a stern look.

(S41) *L'huissier qui saisit   les meubles du   pauvre*
the^bailiff who seize^PRES^3s the furniture of^the poor

n'est   que l'instrument   de la loi humaine dont   il
NEG^be^PRES^3s than the^instrument of the law human   of^which he

n'est   pas responsable.
NEG^be^PRES^3s NEG responsible

"The bailiff who seizes the furniture of a poor man is only an instrument of the human law, for which he is not responsible.

(S42) *Il ne peut   que le plaindre dans son coeur.*
he NEG be^able^PRES^3s than him pity^INF in his heart

He can only pity him in his heart."

(S43) *—Justement! s'écria   saint Pierre.*
justly   himself^cry^out^PS^3s saint Peter

"Exactly!" cried Saint Peter.

(S44) *Celui-ci,   loin d'accorder   une pensée pitoyable au   souvenir*
this^one-here far from^accord^INF a   thought pity^able to^the souvenir

de ses victimes, en   parlait   tout à l'heure   avec une horrible
of his victims of^them speak^IMP^3s all at the^hour with a   horrible

allégresse   et s'y   complaisait   cyniquement.
cheerfulness and himself^there take^pleasure^IMP^3s cynically

"This man, far from sparing a compassionate thought for his victims, was speaking of them a moment ago with a horrible cheerfulness and with cynical pleasure."

(S45) *—Pas du   tout, riposta   Malicorne.*
NEG of^the all   retort^PS^3s Malicorne

"Not at all," retorted Malicorne.

(S46) *Je me   réjouissais   d'avoir   été   toujours exact à*
I myself rejoice^IMP^1s to^have^INF be^PSTPCPL always   exact in

remplir mes fonctions et   aussi de ce que le travail ne
fill^INF my functions and also of this that the work NEG

m'ait   pas manqué.
to^me^have^PRSSBJ^3s NEG lack^PSTPCPL

"I was rejoicing in the fact that I had always been scrupulous in carrying out my duties and also in the fact that I had never lacked work.

(S47) *Est-ce   donc un crime d'aimer   son métier et   de le bien*
       be^PRES^3s-it then a   crime to^love^INF his trade and to it well

       faire?
       do^INF

       Is it then a crime to love one's work and to do it well?"

(S48) *—En général, ce n'est   pas un crime, accorda   Dieu,*
       in   general it NEG^be^PRES^3s NEG a crime accord^PS^3s God

       au   contraire.
       on^the contrary

       "In general, it is not a crime," God admitted, "On the contrary.

(S49) *Votre cas est   assez   particulier;*
       your case be^PRES^3s enough particular

       Your case is somewhat uncommon;

(S50) *mais, enfin, je veux   bien reconnaître   que le jugement de*
       but   finally I want^to^PRES^1s well recognize^INF that the judgment of

       saint Pierre a   été   hâtif.
       saint Peter have^PRES^3s be^PSTPCPL hasty

       but I do want to acknowledge that Saint Peter's judgment was hasty.

(S51) *Voyons   maintenant vos   bonnes oeuvres.*
       see^PRES^1p now   your good   works

       Let's see now your good works.

(S52) *Où   sont-elles?*
       where be^PRES^3p-they

       Where are they?"

(S53) *—Mon Dieu, comme je le disais   tout à l'heure   à saint Pierre, je*
       my   God   as   I it say^IMP^1s all at the^hour to saint Peter I

       suis   mort   sans   rien   devoir   à personne, et
       be^PRES^1s die^PSTPCPL without nothing owe^INF to no^one   and

       j'ai   toujours été   ponctuel aux   offices.
       I^have^PRES^1s always be^PSTPCPL punctual in^the duties

       "My God, as I was just telling Saint Peter, I died without owing anything to anyone, and I've always been assiduous in performing my duties."

(S54) —*Et encore?*
    and besides

"And what else?"

(S55) —*Et encore?*
    and besides

"And what else?

(S56) *Voyons,   je me   souviens   qu'en sortant   de*
see^PRES^1p I myself remember^PRES^1s that^in come^out^PRSPCPL of

la messe, il   y   a   une quinzaine
the mass <dummy^subject> there have^PRES^3s a   fifteen^about

d'années, j'ai   donné   dix sous   à un pauvre.
PART^years I^have^PRES^1s give^PSTPCPL ten pennies to a poor^man

Let's see, as I was coming out of mass around fifteen years ago, I remember giving ten sous to a poor man."

(S57) —*C'est   exact, fit   observer   saint Pierre.*
that^be^PRES^3s exact make^PS^3s observe^INF saint Peter

"That's right," said Saint Peter.

(S58) *C'était   d'ailleurs une pièce fausse.*
it^be^IMP^3s besides   a   coin false

"It was, by the way, a fake coin."

(S59) —*Je suis   tranquille, dit   Malicorne.*
I   be^PRES^1s tranquil say^PS^3s Malicorne

"I'm not worried," said Malicorne.

(S60) *Il aura   bien trouvé   le moyen de la faire   passer.*
he have^FUT^3s well find^PSTPCPL the means of it make^INF pass^INF

"I'm sure he found a way to pass it."

(S61) —*Est-ce   là   tout votre actif?*
be^PRES^3s-this there all   your assets

"Is this then all of your good deeds?"

(S62) —*Mon Dieu, je me   souviens   mal.*
my   God I myself remember^PRES^1s badly

"My God, I don't really remember.

(S63) *On dit   que la main gauche doit   ignorer*
one say^PS^3s that the hand left   should^PRES^3s be^ignorant^of^INF

ce   que   donne   la   main droite.
that which give^PRES^3s the hand right

They say that the left hand shouldn't know what the right hand gives."

(S64) *Il fut   trop facile de vérifier   que ces   belles   paroles ne*
       it be^PS^3s   too easy to verify^INF that these beautiful words NEG

       cachaient   aucune bonne action, ni   aucune   bonne pensée
       hide^IMP^3p not^any good action neither not^any good thought

       dont   une âme se   pût   prévaloir   devant   le
       of^which a   soul himself be^able^IMPSBJ^3s prevail^INF in^front^of the

       tribunal suprême.
       tribunal supreme

       It was only too easy to establish that these pretty words didn't hide any good
       deed or any good thought that a soul might use to prevail before the supreme
       tribunal.

(S65) *Dieu paraissait   très   contrarié.*
       God appear^IMP^3s very annoy^PSTPCPL

       God seemed very annoyed.

(S66) *Parlant   en hébreu, afin   de n'être   pas*
       speak^PRSPCPL in Hebrew in^order to NEG^be^INF NEG

       entendu   de L'huissier, il dit   à saint Pierre:
       understand^PSTPCPL by the^bailiff he say^PS^3s to saint Peter

       Speaking in Hebrew so as not to be understood by the bailiff, he said to Saint
       Peter:

(S67) *—Votre imprudence nous aura   mis   dans un mauvais*
       your   imprudence us   have^FUT^3s put^PSTPCPL in   a bad

       pas.
       step

       "Your rashness seems to have gotten us into a bad situation.

(S68) *Evidemment, cet huissier est   un bonhomme peu*
       evidently   this bailiff be^PRES^3s a good^man little

       intéressant   qui avait   sa place toute trouvée   en Enfer,
       interest^PRSPCPL who have^IMP^3s his place all   find^PSTPCPL in hell

       mais votre accusation portait   à faux et, de plus, vous
       but your accusation carry^IMP^3s to false and of more you

       l'avez   gravement offensé   dans sa fierté
       him^have^PRES^2 gravely   offend^PSTPCPL in   his pride

professionnelle.
professional

Obviously, this bailiff is a run-of-the-mill chap who had his place already
waiting for him in Hell, but your accusation was ill-founded and, what's more,
you wounded his professional pride.

(S69)   *Nous lui   devons   réparation.*
we   to^him owe^PRES^1p reparation

We need to make amends to him.

(S70)   *Et   que   voulez-vous   que je fasse   de   lui?*
and what want^PRES^2-you that I do^PRSSBJ^1s with him

And what do you want me to do with him?

(S71)   *Je ne   peux   pourtant pas lui   ouvrir   les portes de*
I   NEG be^able^PRES^1s however NEG to^him open^INF the doors of

Paradis.
paradise

I certainly can't let him into Heaven.

(S72)   *Ce serait   un scandale.*
that be^COND^3s a   scandal

That would be scandalous.

(S73)   *Alors?*
well^then

So?"

(S74)   *Saint Pierre gardait   un silence maussade.*
saint Peter keep^IMP^3s a   silence sullen

Saint Peter maintained a sullen silence.

(S75)   *S'il   n'avait   tenu   qu'à lui, le sort de L'huissier*
if^it NEG^have^IMP^3s hold^PSTPCPL than^to him the fate of the^bailiff

eût   été   bientôt   réglé.
have^IMPSBJ^3s be^PSTPCPL well^soon regulate^PSTPCPL

If it had only been up to him, the fate of the bailiff would have been quickly
settled.

(S76)   *Le laissant   à sa mauvaise humeur, Dieu se   tourna*
him leave^PRSPCPL to his bad   mood   God himself turn^PS^3s

vers   Malicorne et lui   dit   en bon français:
toward Malicorne and to^him say^PS^3s in good French

Leaving him to his bad temper, God turned to Malicorne and said to him in good French:

(S77)   —*Vous êtes   un méchant, mais l'erreur   de saint Pierre vous*
        you   be^PRES^2 an evil^one but   the^error of saint Peter you

sauve.
save^PRES^3s

"You are an evildoer, but Saint Peter's error has saved you.

(S78)   *Il ne   sera   pas dit   que vous avez   échappé*
        it NEG be^FUT^3s NEG say^PS^3s that you have^PRES^2 escape^PSTPCPL

        à   l'Enfer pour retomber   en   Enfer.
        from the^hell for   re^fall^INF into hell

        It will not be said that you escaped Hell only to fall back into Hell.

(S79)   *Comme vous êtes   indigne   d'entrer   au   Paradis, je*
        as   you   be^PRES^2 un^worthy to^enter^INF into^the paradise I

        vous renvoie   sur la   terre poursuivre votre carrière d'huissier
        you   re^send^PRES^1s on the earth pursue^INF your career of^bailiff

        et   essayer de ressaisir   votre chance de béatitude.
        and try^INF to re^seize^INF your chance of bliss

        As you are unworthy to enter Heaven, I return you to earth to pursue your fortune as a bailiff and to try to find your way to Paradise.

(S80)   *Allez   et   profiter   de   ce sursis   qui vous   est*
        go^PRES^2 and profit^INF from this reprieve which to^you be^PRES^3s

        accordé
        accord^PSTPCPL

        Go and profit from this reprieve which has been given to you."

(S81)   *Le lendemain matin,   en s'éveillant   auprès de son*
        the next^day   morning in himself^awaken^PRSPCPL near   to his

        épouse, Malicorne aurait   pu   croire   qu'il
        spouse Malicorne have^COND^3s be^able^PSTPCPL believe^INF that^he

        avait   rêvé,   mais il ne   s'y   trompa   point
        have^IMP^3s dream^PSTPCPL but   he NEG himself^there fool^PS^3s NEG

        et   réfléchit   aux   moyens de faire   son salut.
        and reflect^PS^3s on^the means of make^INF his salvation

        The next day, on awakening next to his wife, Malicorne might have thought that he had been dreaming, but he didn't make that mistake and he reflected on ways of obtaining his salvation.

(S82) *Il y   pensait   encore lorsqu'il   pénétra   dans son*
       he there think^IMP^3s yet   when^that^he penetrate^PS^3s in   his

       étude, à huit heures.
       study at eight hours

       He was still thinking about this when he entered his study at eight o'clock.

(S83) *Son clerc, le vieux Bourrichon, qui travaillait   avec lui depuis trente*
       his clerk the old   Bourrichon who work^IMP^3s with him since   thirty

       ans, était   déjà   assis   à table.
       years be^IMP^3s already sit^PSTPCPL at table

       His clerk, the old Bourrichon, who had worked with him for thirty years, was
       already seated at the table.

(S84) *—Bourrichon, dit   l'huissier en entrant,   je vous*
       Bourrichon   say^PS^3s the^bailiff in enter^PRSPCPL I you

       augmente   de cinquante francs par mois.
       increase^PRES^1s by fifty   francs per month

       "Bourrichon," said the bailiff as he entered, "I am giving you a raise of fifty
       francs a month."

(S85) *—Vous êtes   trop bon, monsieur Malicorne, protesta*
       you   be^PRES^2 too good Mr.   Malicorne protest^PS^3s

       Bourrichon en joignant   les mains.
       Bourrichon in join^PRSPCPL the hands

       "You are too good, Mr. Malicorne," protested Bourrichon, clasping his hands.

(S86) *Merci bien, monsieur Malicorne.*
       thank well Mr.   Malicorne

       "Thank you very much, Monsieur Malicorne."

(S87) *L'expression   de cette gratitude n'émut   pas le   coeur de*
       the^expression of this   gratitude NEG^move^PS^3s NEG the heart of

       L'huissier.
       the^bailiff

       This expression of gratitude didn't move the heart of the bailiff.

(S88) *Dans un placard, il s'en   fut   prendre un cahier   neuf*
       in   a   cupboard he himself^of^it be^PS^3s take^INF a   notebook new

       et, d'un   trait vertical, partagea   la première page en   deux
       and with^a stroke vertical divide^PS^3s the first   page into two

       colonnes.
       columns

He went over to a cupboard, took out a new notebook, and, with a vertical stroke, divided the first page into two columns.

(S89)   *En tête   de la   colonne de gauche, il   traça   ces   mots   en*
at   head of the   column   of left   he   trace^PS^3s these words in

lettres rondes: «Mauvaises actions», et   dans l'autre,   en regard:
letters round bad   actions   and in   the^other in regard

«Bonnes actions».
good   actions

At the top of the left column, he traced these words in round letters: "Bad Deeds," and, in the opposite column, "Good Deeds."

(S90)   *Il   se   promit   d'être   sévère   à   lui-même et   de*
he himself promise^PS^3s to^be^INF severe with him-self and to

n'oublier   rien   qui   pût   témoigner contre   lui.
NEG^forget^INF nothing that be^able^IMPSBJ^3s testify^INF against him

He resolved to be strict with himself and not to forget anything which could testify against him.

(S91)   *Ce fut   dans cet esprit d'austère   équité qu'il   examina   son*
it   be^PS^3s in   this spirit of^austere equity that^he examine^PS^3s his

emploi   du   temps de ce   début   de matinée.
employment of^the time   of this beginning of morning

It was in this spirit of austere justice that he examined his agenda for this early morning.

(S92)   *Il ne   trouva   rien   à faire   figurer   dans la   colonne*
he NEG find^PS^3s nothing to make^INF represent^INF in   the column

de gauche, et   il écrivit   au   chapitre des   bonnes actions:
of left   and he write^PS^3s in^the chapter of^the good   actions

He didn't find anything to put down in the left column, and he wrote in the "Good Deed" section:

(S93)   *«J'ai,   spontanément, augmenté   de cinquante francs par*
I^have^PRES^1s spontaneously increase^PSTPCPL by fifty   francs per

mois   mon clerc Bourrichon qui   ne   le méritait   pourtant pas.»
month my   clerk Bourrichon who NEG it deserve^IMP^3s however NEG

"I spontaneously gave a raise to my clerk Bourrichon, who, however, didn't deserve it."

(S94)   *Vers   neuf heures, il   eut   la   visite de M. Gorgerin, son*
toward nine hours   he have^PS^3s the visit of Mr. Gorgerin his

meilleur client.
best   client

Around nine o'clock, he had a visit from his best client, Monsieur Gorgerin.

(S95) *C'était   un gros propriétaire possédant   quarante^deux*
this^be^IMP^3s a   large landlord   possess^PRSPCPL forty^two

immeubles dans la ville, et   que le   défaut d'argent   de certains de
buildings in   the city and that the lack   of^money of certain of

ses locataires obligeait   à recourir très souvent au   ministère de
his tenants   oblige^IMP^3s to resort^INF very often   to^the ministry of

Malicorne.
Malicorne

This was a stout landlord who owned forty-two buildings in the city and who
was often obliged, by the negative financial status of some of his tenants, to
make use of Malicorne's services.

(S96) *Cette fois, il venait   l'entretenir   d'une   famille besogneuse*
this   time he come^IMP^3s him^talk^to^INF about^a family   needy

qui était   en retard de deux termes.
that be^IMP^3s in delay by two   terms

This time, he was coming to see Malicorne about a needy family that was two
terms late.

(S97) *—Je ne   peux   plus attendre.*
I   NEG be^able^PRES^1s more wait^INF

"I can't wait any longer.

(S98) *Voilà   six mois   que je me   contente   de   promesses.*
here^is six month that I myself content^PRES^1s with promises

That makes six months now that I've been satisfied with promises.

(S99) *Qu'on   en   finisse.*
that^one of^it finish^PRSSBJ^3s

Let's be done with it."

(S100) *Malicorne, non sans   répugnance, fit   l'effort   de plaider*
Malicorne NEG without repugnance make^PS^3s the^effort to plead^INF

la   cause de ces   mauvais locataires.
the cause of these bad   tenants

Malicorne, not without repugnance, made an effort to plead the cause of these
bad tenants.

(S101)   —*Je me demande si votre intérêt ne serait pas de*
I   myself ask^PRES^1s if your interest NEG be^COND^3s NEG to

leur accorder encore des délais.
to^them accord^INF again PART^the delays

"I wonder if it wouldn't be in your best interests to grant them yet another extension.

(S102) *Leurs meubles ne valent pas quatre sous.*
their furniture NEG be^worth^PRES^3p NEG four pennies

Their furniture isn't worth four sous.

(S103) *Le produit de la vente ne couvrira pas le dixième de votre*
the product of the sale NEG cover^FUT^3s NEG the tenth of your

créance.
debt

The proceeds from the sale would not cover a tenth of what they owe you."

(S104) —*Je le sais bien, soupira Gorgerin.*
I   the know^PRES^1s well sigh^PS^3s Gorgerin

"I know," sighed Gorgerin.

(S105) *J'ai été trop bon.*
I^have^PRES^1s be^PSTPCPL too good

"I've been too kind.

(S106) *On est toujours trop bon.*
one be^PRES^3s always too good

One is always too kind.

(S107) *Ces gens-là en abusent.*
these people-there of^it abuse^PRES^3p

Those people take advantage of it.

(S108) *C'est pourquoi je viens vous demander de faire le*
that^be^PRES^3s why I come^PRES^1s you ask^INF to do^INF the

nécessaire.
necessary

That's why I have come to ask you to do what is necessary.

(S109) *Songez que j'ai cent cinquante et un*
think^PRES^2 that I^have^PRES^1s one^hundred fifty and one

locataires.
tenants

Remember that I have one hundred and fifty-one tenants.

(S110) *Si le   bruit   venait   à   courir   que je suis   bon, je*
if the noise come^IMP^3s to run^INF that I be^PRES^1s good I

n'arriverais   plus à encaisser   seulement la   moitié de mes
NEG^arrive^COND^1s more to collect^INF only   the half   of my

loyers.
rents

If the rumor got started that I was kind-hearted, I wouldn't manage to collect even half of my rent."

(S111) *—C'est   évident, convint   Malicorne.*
that^be^PRES^3s evident agree^PS^3s Malicorne

"That's true," admitted Malicorne.

(S112) *En toutes choses, il faut   considérer   la fin.*
in   all   things   it be^necessary^PRES^3s consider^INF the end

"In all things, you have to consider the end result.

(S113) *Mais, rassurez-vous,   monsieur Gorgerin.*
but   re^assure^PRES^2-yourself Mr.   Gorgerin

But don't worry, Monsieur Gorgerin.

(S114) *Moi qui vois   pas mal de monde, je n'ai*
I   who see^PRES^1s NEG badly of world   I   NEG^have^PRES^1s

entendu   nulle part   que vous étiez   bon.
hear^PSTPCPL no   place that you be^IMP^2 good

I get around quite a lot, and I haven't heard it said anywhere that you were kind-hearted."

(S115) *—Tant   mieux, ma foi.*
so^much better my faith

"Well, that's good."

(S116) *—D'une certaine façon, peut-être, en effet.*
in^a   certain way   perhaps in effect

"In a certain way, perhaps, yes."

(S117) *Malicorne n'osa   pas achever   sa pensée.*
Malicorne NEG^dare^PS^3s NEG finish^INF his thought

Malicorne did not dare complete his thought.

(S118) *Il rêvait   à   la   situation confortable   d'un pécheur*
he dream^IMP^3s of the situation comfort^able of^a sinner

arrivant   devant   le   tribunal de Dieu, précédé   de la
arrive^PRSPCPL in^front^of the tribunal of God precede^PSTPCPL by the

rumeur de toute une ville qui témoignait   de sa bonté.
clamor of all   a   city that testify^IMP^3s of his goodness

He was dreaming of the comfortable situation of a sinner arriving before the
judgment of God, preceded by the noise of a whole town that testified of his
goodness.

(S119) *Après avoir   reconduit   son client jusqu'à   la   porte, il*
after have^INF re^conduct^PS^3s his client as^far^as^to the door he

s'en   fut   tout droit   à la cuisine et, en présence de
himself^of^it be^PS^3s all   straight to the kitchen and in presence of

sa femme épouvantée,   dit   à la   servante:
his wife   appall^PSTPCPL say^PS^3s at the servant

After he had reaccompanied his client to the door, he went straight to the
kitchen and, as his wife stood by, appalled, he said to the servant:

(S120) *—Mélanie, je vous augmente   de cinquante francs par mois.*
Mélanie   I   you increase^PRES^1s by fifty   francs per month

"Mélanie, I am giving you a raise of fifty francs a month."

(S121) *Sans   attendre   les remerciements, il revint   à l'étude*
without wait^for^INF the thanks   he come^back^PS^3s to the^study

et   écrivit   sur son cahier,   dans la   colonne des   bonnes
and write^PS^3s on his notebook in   the column of^the good

actions:
actions

Without waiting to be thanked, he returned to his study and wrote in his
notebook, in the "Good Deeds" column:

(S122) *«J'ai,   spontanément, augmenté   de cinquante francs par*
I^have^PRES^1s spontaneously increase^PSTPCPL by fifty   francs per

mois   ma servante Mélanie qui est   pourtant un souillon.»
month my servant Mélanie who be^PRES^3s however a   slattern

"I spontaneously gave a raise to my servant Mélanie, who is, however, a
slattern."

(S123) *N'ayant   plus personne à augmenter, il s'en*
NEG^have^PRSPCPL more no^one   to increase^INF he himself^of^it

> *alla   dans les bas quartiers de la ville, où   il   visita*
> go^PS^3s in   the low quarters of the city where he visit^PS^3s
>
> *quelques familles pauvres.*
> several   families poor

Having no one else to give a raise to, he went down into the lower districts
of the town and visited several poor families.

(S124) *Les hôtes ne le voyaient   pas entrer   sans   appréhension et*
the hosts NEG the see^IMP^3p NEG enter^INF without apprehension and

> *l'accueillaient   avec une réserve hostile, mais il   se*
> him^greet^IMP^3p with a   reserve hostile but   he himself
>
> *hâtait   de les   rassurer   et laissait   en partant*
> hasten^IMP^3s to them re^assure^INF and leave^IMP^3s in leave^PRSPCPL
>
> *un billet de cinquante francs.*
> a   bill of fifty   francs

It was with apprehension that his hosts watched him enter their homes, and
they greeted him with hostile reserve, but he hastened to reassure them and
left each time a fifty franc note.

(S125) *En général, lorsqu'il   était   sorti,   ses*
in general when^that^he be^IMP^3s go^out^PSTPCPL his

> *obligés   empochaient l'argent   en grommelant:*
> oblige^PSTPCPL^p pocket^IMP^3p the^money in mutter^PRSPCPL

In general, when he had left, his benefactees pocketed the money, grumbling:

(S126) *«Vieux voleur (ou vieux assassin, ou vieux grippe-sou),   il*
old   thief or old   murderer or old   snatch-penny he

> *peut   bien faire   la charité avec tout ce   qu'il*
> be^able^PRES^3s well do^INF the charity with all   that which^he
>
> *a   gagné   sur notre misère.»*
> have^PRES^3s gain^PSTPCPL on our   misery

"Old thief (or old murderer or old Scrooge), he can afford to give some away
with all that he has gained from our misery."

(S127) *Mais c'était   là   plutôt une façon   de parler*
but   that^be^IMP^3s there rather a   manner of speak^INF

> *qu'imposait   la pudeur d'un revirement d'opinion.*
> that^impose^IMP^3s the modesty of^a sudden^turn of^opinion.

But then that was the manner of speaking that was imposed by the shame of
a sudden change of opinion.

(S128) *Au   soir   de sa résurrection, Malicorne avait   inscrit*
by^the evening of his resurrection Malicorne have^IMP^3s enter^PSTPCPL

dans son cahier   douze bonnes actions qui lui   revenaient
in   his notebook twelve good   actions that to^him come^back^IMP^3p

à six cent   francs, et   pas une mauvaise.
to six hundred francs and NEG a   bad^one

The evening of his resurrection, Malicorne had entered twelve good deeds into
his notebook that had cost him six hundred francs, and not one bad deed.

(S129) *Le lendemain et   les jours suivants,   il continua   de*
the next^day and the days follow^PRSPCPL^p he continue^PS^3s to

distribuer   de   l'argent   aux   familles nécessiteuses.
distribute^INF PART the^money to^the families necessitous

The next day and in the days that followed, he continued to distribute money
to needy families.

(S130) *Il s'était   imposé   une moyenne quotidienne de*
he himself^be^IMP^3s impose^PSTPCPL an average daily   of

douze bonnes actions, qu'il   portait   à quinze ou seize   quand
twelve good   actions that^he carry^IMP^3s to fifteen or sixteen when

son foie ou son estomac lui   inspirait   des   inquiétudes.
his liver or his stomach to^him inspire^IMP^3s PART^the anxieties

He had set himself a daily average of twelve good deeds which he increased
to fifteen or sixteen when anxieties over internal ailments inspired him.

(S131) *Une digestion un peu laborieuse de l'huissier valut   ainsi une*
a   digestion a   little laborious of the^bailiff be^worth^PS^3s thus a

nouvelle augmentation de cinquante francs à Bourrichon qui, naguère
new   augmentation of fifty   francs to Bourrichon who recently

encore, redoutait   ce   genre de malaise   dont   il faisait
yet   dread^IMP^3s this type of discomfort of^which he make^IMP^3s

presque toujours les frais.
almost always   the expenses

A case of indigestion was thus worth a new raise of fifty francs to Bourrichon,
who, previously, had dreaded this kind of discomfort, which almost always cost
him dearly.

(S132) *Tant   de   bienfaits ne   pouvaient   passer*
so^many PART kindnesses NEG be^able^IMP^3p pass^INF

inaperçus.
un^perceive^PSTPCPL^p

So many kind deeds could not pass unnoticed.

(S133) *Le bruit courut   en ville que Malicorne préparait   les voies à*
the noise run^PS^3s in city that Malicorne prepare^IMP^3s the ways for

une candidature électorale, car   on le connaissait de   trop
a candidacy electoral because one the know^IMP^3s from too

longue date pour admettre   qu'il   agissait   dans un but
long date for admit^INF that^he act^IMP^3s in a purpose

désintéressé.
dis^interest^PSTPCPL

The rumor ran around in town that Malicorne was preparing the way for an electoral campaign, since people had known him too long to suppose that he was acting out of unselfish motivations.

(S134) *Il eut   un instant de découragement, mais en songeant*
he have^IMPSBJ^3s an instant of discouragement but in think^PRSPCPL

à l'importance   de l'enjeu,   il se   ressaisit   bien vite
of the^importance of the^stakes he himself re^seize^PS^3s well quickly

et   redoubla   de charités.
and re^double^PS^3s of charities

He had a moment of discouragement, but, as he reflected on what was at stake, he quickly shook it off and redoubled his efforts.

(S135) *Au   lieu de borner   sa générosité à des   aumônes aux*
in^the place of limit^INF his generosity to PART^the alms   to^the

particuliers,   il eut   l'idée   de faire   des   dons à
particular^ones he have^PS^3s the^idea of make^INF PART^the gifts to

l'oeuvre des   Dames Patronnesses de la ville, au   curé de   sa
the^work of^the ladies patroness   of the city to^the priest PART his

paroisse, à des   sociétés de secours mutuels, à la   Fraternelle
parish   to PART^the societies of help   mutual to the fraternal

des   pompiers, à l'Amicale   des   anciens élèves du
of^the firemen   to the^friendly^society of^the former students of^the

collège   et   à toutes les oeuvres, chrétiennes ou laïques,
middle^school and to all   the works   Christian or secular

constituées   sous la présidence d'un personnage influent.
constitute^PSTPCPL under the presidency of^a person   influential

Instead of limiting his generosity to gifts to specific individuals, he came up with the idea of giving donations to the Patron Ladies of the city, to the priest of his parish, to mutual assistance societies, to the Brotherhood of Firemen, to the Friendly Society of Former Middle School Students and to all works, whether Christian or secular, which were headed up by some important person.

(S136) *En quatre mois,* *il* *eut* *dépensé* *ainsi près d'un dixième*
in four month he have^PS^3s spend^PSTPCPL thus close to^a tenth

de sa fortune, mais sa réputation était solidement
of his fortune but his reputation be^IMP^3s solidly

établie.
establish^PSTPCPL

Within four months, he had spent close to a tenth of his fortune, but his reputation was solidly established.

(S137) *On le donnait dans toute la ville comme un modèle de charité,*
one him give^IMP^3s in all the city as a model of charity

et son exemple fut si entraînant que les dons se
and his example be^PS^3s so carry^away^PRSPCPL that the gifts himself

mirent à affluer de toutes parts aux entreprises
put^PS^3p to flow^INF from all parts to^the undertakings

philanthropiques, en sorte que les comités directeurs
philanthropic in such^a^way that the committees directors

purent organiser de nombreux banquets où la chère
be^able^PS^3p organise^INF PART numerous banquets where the food

était fine, abondante, et où l'on tenait des
be^IMP^3s fine abundant and where the^one hold^IMP^3s PART^the

propos édifiants.
discourse edify^PRSPCPL^p

The whole town considered him to be a model of kindness, and his example was so irresistible that donations started to flow in from all directions to philanthropic concerns, and the governing boards of these were able to organise numerous banquets where the food was choice and abundant and where all sorts of edifying speeches were made.

(S138) *Les pauvres eux-mêmes ne marchandaient plus leur gratitude à*
the poor themselves NEG haggle^IMP^3p more their gratitude to

Malicorne dont la bonté devint proverbiale.
Malicorne of^which the goodness become^PS^3s proverbial

The poor themselves no longer begrudged Malicorne their gratitude, and his kindness became proverbial.

(S139) *On disait couramment: «Bon comme Malicorne», et il*
one say^IMP^3s currently good as Malicorne and it

arrivait même assez souvent, et de plus en plus, qu'à
arrive^IMP^3s even enough often and from more to more that^for

cette locution, sans trop y penser, on en
this phrase without too^much there think^INF one

substituât   une autre, si étonnante   et   si insolite
substitute^IMPSBJ^3s an other so astonish^PRSPCPL and so bizarre

qu'elle sonnait   à des   oreilles étrangères comme une
that^it sound^IMP^3s to PART^the ears   foreign like   a

plaisanterie un peu agressive.
witticism   a little agressive

They would say, currently, "Kind as Malicorne," and it happened often and
more and more frequently that, without anyone thinking about it too much,
this phrase was replaced by another so astonishing, so bizarre that it sounded
to foreign ears like a sharp witticism.

(S140) *On disait   en effet: «Bon comme un huissier.»*
one say^IMP^3s in effect good as   a bailiff

They would say, "Kind as a bailiff."

(S141) *Malicorne n'eut   plus qu'à   entretenir   cette réputation*
Malicorne NEG^have^PS^3s more than^to maintain^INF this reputation

et, tout en persévérant   dans ses bonnes oeuvres, attendit
and all in persevere^PRSPCPL in   his good works wait^PS^3s

d'un   coeur tranquille que Dieu voulût   bien le   rappeler
from^a heart tranquil that God want^to^IMPSBJ^3s well him recall^INF

à lui.
to him

Malicorne now had only to keep up this reputation, and, as he persevered in
his good works, he waited with a tranquil heart for the time that it would
please God to recall him.

(S142) *Lorsqu'il   apportait   un don à l'oeuvre des   Dames*
when^that^he bring^IMP^3s a gift to the^work of^the ladies

Patronnesses, la présidente, Mme de Saint-Onuphre, lui   disait
patroness   the president Mrs. of Saint-Onuphre to^him say^IMP^3s

avec tendresse:
with tenderness

Whenever he brought a donation for the work of the Patron Ladies, the
president, Madame de Saint-Onuphre, would say to him tenderly,

(S143) *«Monsieur Malicorne, vous êtes   un saint.»*
Mr.   Malicorne you be^PRES^2 a saint

"Monsieur Malicorne, you are a saint."

(S144) *Et il protestait   avec humilité:*
and he protest^IMP^3s with humility

And he would protest with humility,

(S145) *«Oh! madame, un saint, c'est   trop   dire.*
oh   Madam   a   saint   that^be^PRES^3s too^much say^INF

"Oh, Madam, a saint, that's going too far.

(S146) *J'en   suis   encore loin.»*
I^from^it   be^PRES^1s   yet   far

I am still a long ways from that."

(S147) *Sa femme, ménagère pratique et   économe, trouvait   que toute cette*
his wife   housewife practical and frugal   find^IMP^3s that all   this

bonté   revenait   cher.
goodness come^back^IMP^3s expensive

His wife, a thrifty, no-nonsense housewife, found all of this kindness rather
expensive.

(S148) *Elle se   montrait   d'autant   plus   irritée   que la*
she herself show^IMP^3s of^so^much more irritate^PSTPCPL that the

vraie raison de ces   prodigalités ne   lui   échappait   pas.
true reason of these excesses   NEG to^her escape^IMP^3s NEG

She showed herself all the more irritated that the true reason for all these
excesses did not escape her notice.

(S149) *—Tu achètes   ta   part de paradis, disait-elle   assez   crûment,*
you   buy^PRES^1s your part of paradise say^IMP^3s-she enough crudely

mais tu   ne   donnes   pas un sou   pour la   mienne.
but   you NEG give^PRES^2s NEG a   penny for   the mine

"You're buying your place in Heaven," she would say rather crudely, "But
you're not giving a penny for mine.

(S150) *Je reconnais   bien là   ton   égoïsme.*
I   recognize^PRES^1s well there your selfishness

That's just like your selfishness."

(S151) *Malicorne protestait   mollement qu'il   donnait   pour le*
Malicorne protest^IMP^3s weakly   that^he give^IMP^3s for the

plaisir   de donner, mais ce   reproche lui   était   sensible, et
pleasure of give^INF but this reproach to^him be^IMP^3s feel^able and

il   n'avait   pas la   conscience en paix, si bien qu'il
he NEG^have^IMP^3s NEG the conscience in peace so well that^he

autorisa   sa femme à faire   toutes dépenses   qu'elle
authorize^PS^3s his wife   to make^INF all   expenditures that^she

jugerait   utiles pour entrer   au   ciel.
judge^COND^3s useful for   enter^INF into^the sky

Malicorne protested weakly that he gave for the pleasure of giving, but this reproach seemed fair to him, and his conscience bothered him, so that he gave his wife permission to spend as much as she thought necessary to gain her way into Heaven.

(S152) *Elle déclina   cette offre généreuse avec indignation, et   il   ne*
she decline^PS^3s this   offer generous with indignation and he NEG

put   se   défendre   d'en   éprouver   un vif
be^able^PS^3s himself defend^INF from^of^it experience^INF an intense

soulagement.
relief

She indignantly declined this generous offer, and he couldn't help feeling a strong sense of relief.

(S153) *Au   bout d'un an, l'huissier, qui continuait   à tenir*
at^the end of^a year the^bailiff who continue^IMP^3s to keep^INF

registre de ses bonnes actions, en   avait   rempli   six
record of his good   actions of^them have^IMP^3s fill^PSTPCPL six

cahiers   du   format écolier.
notebooks of^the format schoolboy

By the end of a year, the bailiff, who continued to keep a record of his good deeds, had filled up six elementary school notebooks with them.

(S154) *à chaque instant, il les   sortait   de leur   tiroir, les*
at each   instant he them take^out^IMP^3s of their drawer them

soupesait   avec bonheur et   parfois   s'attardait   à
weigh^in^hand^IMP^3s with bliss   and sometimes himself^delay in

les   feuilleter.
them page^through^INF

He would constantly take them out of their drawer, weigh them blissfully in his hand and sometimes linger to thumb through their pages.

(S155) *Rien   n'était   réconfortant   comme la vue de toutes*
nothing NEG^be^IMP^3s comfort^PRSPCPL like   the view of all

ces   pages, où   les bonnes oeuvres s'inscrivaient   en colonnes
these pages where the good   works themself^enter^IMP^3p in columns

serrées,   à côté des   grandes marges blanches, dont   la
squeeze^PSTPCPL to side of^the large   margins white   of^which the

plupart   étaient   vierges de mauvaises actions.
greater^part be^IMP^3p virgin of bad   actions

Nothing was as reassuring as the sight of all those pages with their tightly squeezed columns of good deeds next to wide white margins which were for the most part blank, pure of any bad deeds.

(S156) *Malicorne, avec un avant-goût   de béatitude, rêvait   à l'heure*
Malicorne with a   before-taste of bliss   dream^IMP^3s of the^hour

où   il comparaîtrait,   chargé   de ce bagage
where he appear^in^court^COND^3s charge^PSTPCPL with this baggage

imposant.
impose^PRSPCPL

Malicorne, with a foretaste of heavenly bliss, dreamed of the day when he would appear above, laden with this impressive load.

(S157) *Un matin   qu'il   venait   de   saisir   les meubles d'un*
a   morning that^he come^IMP^3s from seize^INF the furniture of^an

chômeur,   l'huissier, tandis qu'il   marchait   par   les
unemployed^man the^bailiff while that^he walk^IMP^3s through the

ruelles du   bas quartier, se   sentit   troublé   et
alleys of^the low quarter himself feel^PS^3s disturb^PSTPCPL and

inquiet.
anxious

One morning as he had just taken the furniture of a jobless man and was walking through the alleys of the lower quarter, the bailiff suddenly found himself feeling disturbed and anxious.

(S158) *C'était   une espèce d'incertitude   poignante et   mélancholique ne*
it^be^IMP^3s a   type   of^uncertainty agonizing and melancholy   NEG

se   rapportant   à aucun   objet précis   et
itself refer^PRSPCPL to not^any object specific and

qu'il   ne lui   souvenait   pas d'avoir
that^ < dummy^subject > NEG to^him remember^IMP^3s NEG to^have^INF

jamais éprouvée.
ever   experience^PSTPCPL

It was a type of uncertainty, agonizing and melancholy, that didn't seem related to any particular object and that he didn't remember ever having experienced before.

(S159) *Pourtant, il avait   accompli   son devoir sans   peur*
however he have^IMP^3s accomplish^PSTPCPL his duty   without fear

et   sans   vaine pitié, et   après l'opération,   en faisant
and without vain pity   and after the^operation in make^PRSPCPL

au   chômeur   la   charité d'un billet de cinquante francs, il
to^the unemployed^man the charity of^a bill   of fifty   francs he

n'avait   même pas été   ému.
NEG^have^IMP^3s even   NEG be^PSTPCPL move^PSTPCPL

However, he had accomplished his duty without fear and without vain pity and
when, after the operation, he had given the unemployed man a fifty franc bill,
he had not even been moved.

(S160) Rue de la Poterne, il franchit   le   seuil   d'une vieille maison
street of the Poterne he   cross^PS^3s the threshold of^an old   house

de misère, humide et puante,   qui appartenait   à son client,
of poverty damp   and stink^PRSPCPL that belong^IMP^3s to his client

M. Gorgerin.
Mr. Gorgerin

On Poterne Street, he entered a dank and smelly old tenement house
belonging to his client, Mr. Gorgerin.

(S161) Il la connaissait   de   longue date pour avoir   instrumenté
he it know^IMP^3s from long   date for   have^INF take^action^PSTPCPL

contre plusieurs locataires, et il y   était   venu   la
against several   tenants   and he there be^IMP^3s come^PSTPCPL the

veille distribuer   quelques aumônes.
eve   distribute^INF some   alms

He had known the place a long time since he had acted against several
tenants, and he had just come there the day before to give some alms.

(S162) Il lui   restait   à visiter   le troisième étage.
it to^him remain^IMP^3s to visit^INF the third   floor

It remained for him to visit the third floor.

(S163) Après avoir   suivi   un couloir obscur, aux   murailles
after have^INF follow^PSTPCPL a   corridor dark   with^the high^walls

poisseuses et grimpé   trois rampes, il déboucha   dans une
sticky   and climb^PSTPCPL three inclines he emerge^PS^3s in   a

étrange lumière de grenier.
strange light   of attic

After he had walked down a dark corridor with sticky walls and climbed three
flights of stairs, he came out into an area of strange attic lighting.

(S164) Le troisième et   dernier étage n'était   éclairé   que par
the third   and last   floor NEG^be^IMP^3s light^PSTPCPL than by

une lucarne   *qui s'ouvrait*   *dans un renfoncement du*
an   attic^window   that   itself^open^IMP^3s   in   a   recess   of^the

toit mansardé.
roof mansard

The third and last floor was only lit by an attic window that opened into a recess of the mansard roof.

(S165)   *Malicorne, un peu essoufflé*   *par*   *la montée, s'arrêta*
Malicorne   a   little   wind^PSTPCPL   through   the   ascent   himself^stop^PS^3s

un instant à examiner   *les lieux.*
an instant to examine^INF   the places

Malicorne, a little winded from the climb, stopped a moment to examine his surroundings.

(S166)   *Le plâtre des*   *cloisons*   *mansardées, sous*   *l'effet*   *de*
the plaster of^the   partitions mansard   under the^effect of

l'humidité,   *formait*   *des*   *boursouflures dont*   *plusieurs*
the^dampness form^IMP^3s   PART^the   swellings   of^which several

avaient   *éclaté,*   *laissant*   *apparaître, comme un fond*
have^IMP^3p burst^PSTPCPL allow^PRSPCPL appear^INF like   a   bottom

d'abcès,   *le bois noir et*   *pourri*   *d'un chevron ou du*
of^abscess the wood black and rot^PSTPCPL of^a rafter   or   of^the

lattis.
lattice

The plaster of the mansard roof, under the effect of the humidity, formed blisters. Several of these had burst, revealing, like the bottom of an abscess, the black rotted wood of a rafter or of the lattice.

(S167)   *Sous la lucarne,*   *une cuvette de fer*   *et*   *une serpillière*
under the attic^window a   basin   of iron and a   thick^rag

posées   *à même le plancher que ces*   *précautions ne*
lay^PSTPCPL on even   the floor   that these precautions NEG

protégeaient   *sans*   *doute pas suffisamment des*   *infiltrations*
protect^IMP^3p without doubt NEG sufficiently   from^the infiltrations

d'eau   *de pluie, car*   *il était*   *rongé*   *et*   *vermoulu*
of^water of rain   because it be^IMP^3s gnaw^PSTPCPL and worm^eaten

et   *avait,*   *par endroits, le moelleux d'un tapis.*
and have^IMP^3s in   places   the downy   of^a carpet

Under the window, an iron basin and a thick rag lay directly on the floor, which, unprotected by these precautions (from the rainwater), was gnawed and worm-eaten and had, in places, the downiness of a carpet.

(S168) *Ni   l'aspect   de ce   palier   sombre et   étroit,   ni   le*
neither the^appearance of this landing somber and narrow neither the

relent   fade   qu'on   y   respirait,   n'avaient   de
stale^smell insipid that^one there breathe^IMP^3s NEG^have^IMP^3p with

quoi surprendre   l'huissier qui en   avait   vu
what surprise^INF the^bailiff who of^them have^IMP^3s see^PSTPCPL

bien d'autres   au   cours de sa carrière.
many of^others in^the course of his career

Neither the appearance of this somber, narrow landing nor the insipid, musty
smell that one breathed there held any surprise for the bailiff, who had seen
many others like this in the course of his career.

(S169) *Pourtant, son inquiétude était   devenue   plus*
however his anxiety   be^IMP^3s become^PSTPCPL more

lancinante,   et   il lui   semblait   qu'elle fût   sur le
twinge^PRSPCPL and it to^him seem^IMP^3s that^it be^IMPSBJ^3s on the

point de prendre   un sens.
NEG of take^INF a   sense

However, his anxiety had become more piercing, and it seemed to him that he
was about to learn what it meant.

(S170) *Il entendit   pleurer un enfant dans l'un   des   deux logements*
he hear^PS^3s cry^INF a   child in   the^one of^the two   lodgings

qui ouvraient   sur le palier, mais ne   sut   reconnaître
that open^IMP^3p on the landing but NEG know^PS^3s recognize^INF

avec certitude de   quel   côté venait   la voix, et   frappa
with certainty from which side come^IMP^3s the voice and knock^PS^3s

au   hasard   à l'une   des   deux portes.
at^the random on the^one of^the two   doors

He heard a child crying in one of the two apartments that opened on the
landing. Unable to determine with certainty which side the voice was coming
from, he knocked at random on one of the two doors.

(S171) *Le logement était   de deux pièces en enfilade, étroites comme un*
the lodging be^IMP^3s of two rooms in string   narrow like   a

couloir, et la première, qui   ne recevait   de jour que
corridor and the first   which NEG receive^IMP^3s of day than

par   la porte vitrée   de communication, était   encore
through the door window^PSTPCPL of communication be^IMP^3s yet

plus sombre que le palier.
more somber than the landing

The apartment was composed of two rooms as narrow as the corridor. The first, which only received light through the window of the inside door, was even darker than the landing.

(S172) *Une femme mince, au   visage très jeune, mais fatigué,*
a   woman slender with^the face   very young   but   tire^PSTPCPL

accueillit   Malicorne.
greet^PS^3s   Malicorne

A slender woman, with a very young but tired face, welcomed Malicorne.

(S173) *Un enfant de deux ans   se   tenait   dans ses jupes, les yeux*
a   child of two   years himself hold^IMP^3s in   her skirts the eyes

humides et   regardant   le visiteur avec une curiosité qui,
damp   and look^at^PRSPCPL the visitor with a   curiosity which

déjà,   lui   faisait   oublier   son chagrin.
already to^him make^IMP^3s forget^INF his sadness

A two year old child with damp eyes held onto her skirts and studied the visitor with a curiosity that was already making him forget his sadness.

(S174) *La seconde pièce, dans laquelle   fut   introduit   l'huissier,*
the second room in   the^which be^PS^3s introduce^PSTPCPL the^bailiff

était   meublée   d'un   lit   de sangle,   d'une   petite table
be^IMP^3s furnish^PSTPCPL with^a bed of cloth^band with^a small table

en bois   blanc, de   deux chaises et   d'une   vieille machine à
in wood white with two chairs and with^an old   machine for

coudre   placée   devant   la fenêtre mansardée qui
sew^INF place^PSTPCPL in^front^of the window mansard   which

donnait   sur des   toits.
give^IMP^3s on PART^the roofs

The second room, into which the bailiff was led, was furnished with a cloth strap bed, a little white wood table, two chairs and an old sewing machine, which had been placed in front of the mansard window that looked out onto roofs.

(S175) *La misère   de cet intérieur n'offrait   rien   non plus*
the poverty of this interior NEG^offer^IMP^3s nothing NEG more

qu'il   n'eût   déjà   vu   ailleurs;
than^he NEG^have^IMPSBJ^3s already see^PSTPCPL elsewhere

The poverty of this interior did not present anything that he had not already seen elsewhere.

(S176) *mais pour la   première fois de sa vie, Malicorne se   sentait*
but for the first   time in his life Malicorne himself feel^IMP^3s

intimidé   *en entrant*   *chez*   *un pauvre.*
intimidate^PSTPCPL in enter^PRSPCPL the^place^of a poor^man

But for the first time in his life, Malicorne was feeling intimidated in entering the house of a poor person.

(S177) *Habituellement, ses visites de charité étaient*   *des*   *plus brèves.*
habitually   his visits of charity be^IMP^3p PART^the most brief

Usually, his charity visits were very brief.

(S178) *Sans*   *s'asseoir,*   *il posait*   *quelques questions précises,*
without himself^sit^INF he lay^IMP^3s several questions specific

débitait   *une formule d'encouragement et,*   *lâchant*   *son*
utter^IMP^3s a phrase of^encouragement and let^go^PRSPCPL his

aumône, prenait   *aussitôt la porte.*
alm   take^IMP^3s as^soon the door

Without sitting down, he would ask several specific questions, utter an encouraging phrase, and, dropping his alm, would immediately head out the door.

(S179) *Cette fois, il*   *ne*   *savait*   *plus très bien pourquoi il*   *était*
this time he NEG know^IMP^3s more very well why he be^IMP^3s

venu   *et ne pensait*   *plus à mettre la main à son*
come^PSTPCPL and NEG think^IMP^3s more to put^INF the hand to his

portefeuille.
wallet

This time he wasn't really sure why he had come, and he didn't think to reach for his billfold.

(S180) *Les idées tremblaient*   *dans sa tête et les paroles sur ses lèvres.*
the ideas tremble^IMP^3p in his head and the words on his lips

His ideas trembled in his head and his words on his lips.

(S181) *Il osait*   *à peine lever les yeux sur la petite couturière*
he dare^IMP^3s with difficulty lift^INF the eyes on the small seamstress

en songeant   *à sa profession d'huissier.*
in think^PRSPCPL of his profession of^bailiff

Conscious of his position as a bailiff he hardly dared to lift his eyes upon the little seamstress.

(S182) *De son côté, elle n'était*   *pas moins intimidée,*
from her side she NEG^be^IMP^3s NEG less intimidate^PSTPCPL

quoique sa réputation d'homme charitable lui   *fût*
although his reputation of^man charity^able to^her be^IMPSBJ^3s

connue   depuis longtemps.
know^PSTPCPL since   long^time

As for her, she was no less intimidated, even though she had known of his reputation as a charitable man for a long time.

(S183) *L'enfant fit   presque tous les frais   de l'entretien.*
the^child make^PS^3s almost   all   the expenses of the^conversation

The child was the one who carried the conversation.

(S184) *D'abord   craintif, il ne   tarda   pas à s'apprivoiser   et,*
at^approach fearful   he NEG delay^PS^3s NEG to himself^tame^INF and

de lui-même, monta   sur les genoux de Malicorne.
of him-self   ascend^PS^3s on the knees   of Malicorne

At first fearful, he didn't take long to get used to Malicorne, and to climb up on Malicorne's knees on his own.

(S185) *Celui-ci   eut   un regret si vif   de n'avoir   pas*
this^one-here have^PS^3s a   regret so intense to NEG^have^INF NEG

de   bonbons qu'il   sentit   une petite envie de pleurer.
PART candies   that^he feel^PS^3s a   small desire to cry^INF

Malicorne was so sorry that he hadn't brought any candy that he felt a little bit like crying.

(S186) *Soudain, on entendit   frapper   rudement à la   porte, comme à*
suddenly one hear^PS^3s knock^INF roughly   at the door   as   with

coups de canne.
blows of cane

Suddenly, there was heard a loud rapping on the door, as if someone were rapping with a cane.

(S187) *La couturière parut   bouleversée   et   passa*
the seamstress appear^PS^3s throw^into^confusion^PSTPCPL and pass^PS^3s

dans l'autre   pièce dont   elle ferma   la   porte de
in   the^other room of^which she close^PS^3s the door of

communication.
communication

The seamstress appeared overwhelmed. She went into the other room and closed the connecting door.

(S188) *—Alors? dit   une grosse voix rogue, que Malicorne reconnut*
well   say^PS^3s a   strong voice gruff that Malicorne recognize^PS^3s

pour être　　celle　　de Gorgerin.
for　be^INF　that^one of Gorgerin

"Well?" said a loud gruff voice, that Malicorne recognized as that of Gorgerin.

(S189) *Alors?*
well

"Well?

(S190) *J'espère　　　que c'est　　　pour aujourd'hui?*
I^hope^PRES^1s that it^be^PRES^3s for　today

I hope that today is the day?"

(S191) *La réponse　parvint　　à l'huissier　comme un murmure indistinct,*
the response reach^PS^3s to the^bailiff as　　a　murmur　indistinct

mais le　sens　　était　　trop facile à saisir.
but　the meaning be^IMP^3s too　easy　to seize^INF

The answer came to the bailiff only as an indistinct murmur, but the meaning was easy enough to grasp.

(S192) *Gorgerin se　　mit　　à rugir　　d'une voix terrible qui*
Gorgerin himself put^PS^3s to roar^INF with^a voice terrible that

effraya　　l'enfant et　dut　　emplir toute la　maison:
frighten^INF the^child and must^PS^3s fill^INF all　the house

Gorgerin started to roar in a terrible voice that frightened the child and filled the entire house:

(S193) *—Ah! non!*
ah　　no

"Oh, no!

(S194) *J'en　ai　　　assez, moi!*
I^of^it have^PRES^1s enough myself

I've had enough!

(S195) *Vous ne　me paierez　plus　avec des　　balivernes.*
you NEG me pay^FUT^2 more with PART^the nonsense

You won't pay me anymore with nonsense.

(S196) *Je veux　　　mon argent.*
I　want^PRES^1s my　money

I want my money.

(S197) *Donnez-moi   mon argent, et   tout de suite!*
give^PRES^2-me my   money and all   ?   following

Give me my money, and give it to me now!

(S198) *Allons,   montrez-moi   où   vous mettez   vos   économies.*
go^PRES^1p show^PRES^2-me where you   put^PRES^2 your savings

Go on, show me where you put your savings.

(S199) *Je veux   les   voir.*
I   want^to^PRES^1s them see^INF

I want to see them."

(S200) *Dans un autre temps, Malicorne eût   admiré   en*
in   an other time   Malicorne have^IMPSBJ^3s admire^PSTPCPL in

connaisseur l'entrain avec lequel   Gorgerin menait   la   rude
connoisseur the^spirit with the^which Gorgerin conduct^IMP^3s the rough

besogne qui   consiste   à encaisser   les loyers des   pauvres.
task   which consist^PRES^3s of collect^INF the rents of^the poor

In another time, Malicorne would have admired as a connoisseur the spirit
with which Gorgerin conducted the rough job of collecting rent from the poor.

(S201) *Mais il éprouvait   le même sentiment de crainte qui*
but   he experience^IMP^3s the same feeling   of fear   that

faisait   battre   le coeur de l'enfant réfugié   dans
make^IMP^3s beat^INF the heart of the^child take^refuge^PSTPCPL in

ses bras.
his arms

But the child had taken refuge in his arms and Malicorne was experiencing the
same fear that was making the child's heart pound.

(S202) *—Allons,   sortez   votre argent! clamait   Gorgerin.*
go^PRES^1p get^out^PRES^2 your money shout^IMP^3s Gorgerin

"Go ahead, get out your money!" Gorgerin was shouting.

(S203) *Donnez-le,   ou je saurez   bien le trouver, moi!*
give^PRES^2-it or I know^PRES^2 well it find^INF myself

"Give it up or I'll go find it myself!"

(S204) *L'huissier se   leva   et, posant   l'enfant sur la chaise,*
the^bailiff himself lift^PS^3s and lay^PRSPCPL the^child on the chair

passa   dans l'autre   pièce sans   intention précise.
pass^PS^3s in   the^other room without intention particular

The bailiff got up and, placing the child on the chair, went into the other room without any specific intention.

(S205)　—*Tiens!*　　*s'écria*　　　　　*Gorgerin.*
hold^PRES^2s himself^cry^out^PS^3s Gorgerin

"Well, look!" cried Gorgerin.

(S206)　*J'allais*　　*parler*　　*du*　　*loup, et*　*le*　*voilà*　*qui*
I^go^IMP^1s speak^INF of^the wolf and him here^is that

sort　　　　　　*du*　　*bois.*
come^out^PRES^3s of^the wood

"I was going to speak of the wolf, and there he is coming out of the woods."

(S207)　—*Décampez!*　　*ordonna*　　　*l'huissier.*
get^out^PRES^2 order^PS^3s the^bailiff

"Get out!" ordered the bailiff.

(S208)　*Interloqué,*　　　　　*Gorgerin le*　*considérait*　　*avec des*
make^speechless^PSTPCPL Gorgerin him consider^IMP^3s with PART^the

yeux stupides.
eyes stupid

Speechless, Gorgerin stared at him stupidly.

(S209)　—*Décampez!*　*répéta*　　　*Malicorne.*
get^out^PRES^2 repeat^PS^3s Malicorne

"Get out!" repeated Malicorne.

(S210)　—*Voyons,*　*vous perdez*　　*la*　*tête.*
see^PRES^1p you lost^PRES^2 the head

"Look, man, you're losing your mind.

(S211)　*Je suis*　　　*le*　*propriétaire.*
I be^PRES^1s the landlord

I am the landlord."

(S212)　*Effectivement, Malicorne perdait*　　*la*　*tête, car*　*il*　*se*
effectively　　　Malicorne lost^IMP^3s the head because he himself

rua　　　*sur Gorgerin et*　*le*　*jeta*　　　*hors*　*du*　*logis*　*en*
fling^PS^3s on Gorgerin and him throw^PS^3s outside of^the house in

vociférant:
yell^PRSPCPL

As a matter of fact, Malicorne was losing his mind, because he flung himself at Gorgerin and threw him out of the apartment, yelling:

(S213) —*Un sale cochon de propriétaire, oui.*
a   dirty pig   of landlord   yes

"A filthy swine of a landlord, yes.

(S214) *A bas les propriétaires!*
to low the landlords

Down with landlords!

(S215) *A bas les propriétaires!*
to low the landlords

Down with landlords!"

(S216) *Craignant   pour sa vie, Gorgerin tira   un revolver et,*
fear^PRSPCPL for   his life Gorgerin pull^PS^3s a   revolver and

ajustant   l'huissier, l'étendit   roide mort   sur
aim^at^PRSPCPL the^bailiff him^spread^out^PS^3s ?   die^PSTPCPL on

le petit palier, à côté de la cuvette et de la serpillière.
the small landing to side of the basin and of the thick^rag

Fearing for his life, Gorgerin pulled out a revolver and, taking aim at the bailiff, laid him out stone dead on the little landing, next to the basin and the rag.

(S217) *Dieu se   trouvait   à passer   par la salle d'audience,*
God himself find^IMP^3s to pass^INF by the room of^audience

lorsque   Malicorne fut   admis   à comparaître.
when^that Malicorne be^PS^3s admit^PSTPCPL to appear^in^court^INF

God happened to be passing by the audience hall when Malicorne was admitted for arraignment.

(S218) —*Ah! dit-il,   voici   revenir   notre huissier.*
ah   say^PRES^3s-he here^is come^back^INF our   bailiff

"Ah," said He, "Here is our bailiff back again.

(S219) *Et comment s'est-il   comporté?*
and how   himself^be^PRES^3s-he behave^PSTPCPL

And how has he behaved?"

(S220) —*Ma foi, répondit   saint Pierre, je vois   que son compte*
my   faith answer^PS^3s saint Peter I see^PRES^1s that his account

ne sera   pas long à régler.
NEG be^FUT^3s NEG long to regulate^INF

"My faith," answered Saint Peter, "I see that his account won't take long to settle."

(S221) —*Voyons   un peu   ses bonnes oeuvres.*
see^PRES^1p a   little his good   works

"Let's have a look at his good works."

(S222) —*Oh! ne   parlons   pas de ses bonnes oeuvres.*
oh   NEG speak^PRES^1p NEG of his good   works

"Oh! let's not talk about his good works.

(S223) *Il   n'en   a   qu'une   à son actif.*
he NEG^of^them have^PRES^3s but^one to his assets

He only has one to his credit."

(S224) *Ici,   saint Pierre considéra   Malicorne avec un sourire*
here saint Peter consider^PS^3s Malicorne with a   smile

attendri.
make^tender^PSTPCPL

And here, Saint Peter considered Malicorne with a tender smile.

(S225) *l'huissier voulut   protester   et faire   état de toutes les*
the^bailiff want^to^PS^3s protest^INF and make^INF state of all   the

bonnes actions inscrites   dans ses cahiers,   mais le   saint ne
good   actions enter^PSTPCPL in   his notebooks but   the saint NEG

lui   laissa   pas la parole.
to^him leave^PS^3s NEG the word

The bailiff wanted to protest and cite all of the good deeds recorded in his notebooks, but the saint wouldn't let him say anything.

(S226) —*Oui, une seule bonne oeuvre, mais qui   est   de poids.*
yes   an only good work   but which be^PRES^3s of weight

"Yes, a single good work, but it's a weighty one.

(S227) *Il   a   crié,   lui, un huissier: «A bas les propriétaires.»*
he have^PRES^3s cry^PSTPCPL he a bailiff   to low the landlords

He, a bailiff, cried out: 'Down with landlords'."

(S228) —*Que c'est   beau,   murmura   Dieu.*
how   that^be^PRES^3s beautiful murmur^PS^3s God

"How beautiful," murmured God.

(S229) *Que c'est   beau.*
how that^be^PRES^3s beautiful

"How beautiful."

(S230) —*Il l'a   crié   par deux fois, et il   en   est*
        he   it^have^PRES^3s cry^PSTPCPL for two   time and he of^it be^PRES^3s

        mort   au   moment même où   il   défendait   une
        die^PSTPCPL at^the   moment even where he   defend^IMP^3s a

        pauvresse contre la   férocité de son propriétaire.
        poor   against the ferocity of her landlord

        "He shouted it two times and died for it at the very moment when he was
        defending a poor woman against the ferocity of her landlord."

(S231) *Dieu, émerveillé,   commanda   aux   anges de jouer,   en*
        God   marvel^PSTPCPL command^PS^3s to^the angels to play^INF in

        l'honneur de Malicorne, du   luth, de   la   viole, du
        the^honor of Malicorne PART^the   lute PART the viol   PART^the

        hautbois et   du   flageolet.
        oboe   and PART^the flageolet

        God, completely amazed, commanded the angels to play, in honor of
        Malicorne, the lute, the viol, the oboe and the flageolet.

(S232) *Ensuite, il fit   ouvrir   les portes du   ciel à deux battants,*
        then   he make^PS^3s open^INF the doors to^the sky at two ?

        comme cela se   fait   pour les déshérités,   les
        as   that itself do^PRES^3s for the disinherit^PSTPCPL^p the

        clochards, les claque-dents et   les condamnés à   mort.
        hobos   the clap-teeth   and the condemned to death

        Then he commanded the angels to open wide the gates of Heaven as is done
        for the disinherited, the tramps, the trembling and the condemned to death.

(S233) *Et l'huissier, porté   par un air de musique, entra*
        and the^bailiff carry^PSTPCPL by an air of music   enter^PS^3s

        au   Paradis avec un rond de lumière sur la   tête.
        into^the   paradise with a round of light   on the head

        And the bailiff, carried by strains of music, entered Heaven with a circle of
        light upon his head.

References

Abrate, Jayne. 1983. An approach to teaching the past tenses in French. The French Review 56:4.

Allen, Robert Livingston. 1966. The verb system of present-day American English. Janua linguarum 34. The Hague: Mouton.

Aymé, Marcel. 1943. L'huissier. Le passe-muraille, 192–204. Paris: Editions Gallimard.

Balzac, Honoré de. 1973. Le père Goriot, extraits, tome 1. Paris: Librairie Larousse.

Bronzwaer, W. J. M. 1970. Tense in the novel: An investigation of some potentialities of linguistic criticism. Groningen, The Netherlands: Wolters-Noordhoff Publishing.

Camus, Albert. 1947. La peste. Paris: Librairie Gallimard.

Chafe, Wallace L. 1970. Meaning and the structure of language. Chicago: The University of Chicago Press.

Comrie, Bernard. 1976. Aspect: An introduction to the study of verbal aspect and related problems. Cambridge: Cambridge University Press.

Cox, Thomas J. 1982. The inchoative aspect in French. The French Review 56:228–40.

Dahl, Osten. 1981. On the definition of the telic-atelic (bounded-non-bounded) distinction. In Philip J. Tedeschi and Annie Zaenen (eds.), Syntax and semantics 14: Tense and aspect, 79–90. New York: Academic Press.

———. 1985. Tense and aspect systems. Oxford: Basil Blackwell.

Desclés, Jean-Pierre and Zlatka Guentchéva. 1987. Fonctions discursives: passé simple et imparfait. Le texte comme objet philosophique: présentation de Jean Greisch, 111–37. (Institut Catholique de Paris Faculté de Philosophie, 12.) Paris: Beauchesne.

133

van Dijk, Teun A. 1977. Text and context: Explanations in the semantics and pragmatics of discourse. London: Longman.

Dumas, Alexandre (père). 1943. Les trois mousquetaires. Paris: Editions Louis Conard.

Dumas Alexandre (fils). 1983. La dame aux camélias. Paris: Le Livre de Poche.

Faucher, Eugène. 1967. Les temps verbaux du français et de l'allemand transmettent-ils des informations chronologique? Reflexions sur tempus de H. Weinrich. Etudes Germaniques 3:359–67.

Flaubert, Gustave. 1965. Un coeur simple. In Morris Bishop (ed.), A survey of French literature 2: The nineteenth and twentieth centuries, 150–67. New York: Harcourt Brace Jovanovich.

———. 1972. Madame Bovary. Paris: Editions Gallimard.

Garey, Howard B. 1957. Verbal aspect in French. Language 33:91–110.

Givón, Talmy, ed. 1979. Syntax and Semantics 12: Discourse and syntax. New York: Academic Press.

———. 1984. Syntax: A functional-typological introduction, 1. Amsterdam: John Benjamins.

Grammaire Larousse du français contemporain. 1964. Jean-Claude Chevalier, Claire Blanche-Benveniste, Michel Arrivé, and Jean Peytard. Paris: Librairie Larousse.

Grévisse, Maurice. 1969. Précis de grammaire française. Paris-Gembloux: Editions Duculot.

———. 1980. Le bon usage: grammaire française avec des remarques sur la langue française d'aujourd'hui. Paris-Gembloux: Editions Duculot.

Grimes, Joseph E. 1975. The thread of discourse. The Hague: Mouton.

Grobe, Edwin P. 1967. Passé simple versus imparfait. The French Review 41:344–56.

Halliday, M. A. K. 1967. Notes on transitivity and theme in English, 2. Journal of Linguistics 3:199–244.

Hopper, Paul J. 1979a. Aspect and foregrounding in discourse. In Givón 1979, 213–41.

———. 1979b. Some observations on the typology of focus and aspect in narrative language. Studies in Language 3:37–64.

——— and Sandra Thompson. 1980. Transitivity in grammar and discourse. Language 56:251–99.

Imbs, Paul. 1960. L'emploi des temps verbaux en français moderne. Paris: Librairie C. Klincksieck.

Kenny, Anthony. 1963. Action, emotion and will. London: Routledge and Kegan Paul.

La Fontaine. 1929. Fables, ed. by L. Clément. 24th edn. Paris: Colin.

Lasserre, E. and J. Grandjean. 1948. Etude du verbe. Lausanne: Librairie Payot.

Leblanc, Maurice. 1967. La demoiselle aux yeux verts. Paris: Claude Leblanc et Librairie Générale Française. (Livre de Poche)

Longacre, Robert E. 1968. Discourse, paragraph, and sentence structure in selected Philippine languages. Summer Institute of Linguistics Publications 11. Santa Ana: Summer Institute of Linguistics.

―――. 1972. Hierarchy and universality of discourse constituents in New Guinea languages. Washington: Georgetown University Press.

―――. 1976. 'Mystery' particles and affixes. Papers from the twelfth regional meeting, Chicago Linguistic Society, ed. by S. S. Mufwene, C. A. Walker, and S. B. Smith, 468–75. Chicago: Chicago Linguistic Society.

―――. 1981. A spectrum and profile approach to discourse analysis. Text 1:337–59.

―――. 1983. The grammar of discourse. New York: Plenum Press.

―――. 1990. Storyline concerns and word order typology in east and west Africa. Los Angeles: James S. Coleman African Studies Center and the Department of Linguistics-UCLA.

Martin, Robert. 1971. Temps et aspect: essai sur l'emploi des temps narratifs en moyen français. Paris: Editions Klincksieck.

Mourelatos, Alexandre P. D. 1978. Events, processes and states. Linguistics and Philosophy 2:415–34.

―――. 1981. Events, processes and states. In Philip J. Tedeschi and Annie Zaenen (eds.), System and semantics 14: Tense and aspect, 191–212. New York: Academic Press.

Murdoch, Iris. 1964. The Italian girl. London: Chatto and Windus.

Pagnol, Marcel. 1985. La gloire de mon père. Edinburgh: Thomas Nelson.

Reid, Wallis. 1977. The quantitative validation of a grammatical hypothesis: The passé simple and the imparfait. In Judy Anne Kegl, David Nash and Annie Zaenen (eds.), Proceedings of the Seventh Annual Meeting of the North Eastern Linguistic Society, 315–33.

Sten, Holger. 1952. Les temps du verbe fini (indicatif) en français moderne. Historisk-filosofiske Meddelelser, bind 33, nr. 3. Copenhagen: Ejnar Munksgaard. A publication of Det Kongelige Danske Videnskabernes Selskab.

Thomas, Jose Pushpalayam. 1989. Prominence in French discourse. Ph.D. dissertation, The University of Texas at Arlington.

Vendler, Zeno. 1957. Verbs and times. Language 56:143–60.

―――. 1967. Linguistics in philosophy. Ithaca, New York: Cornell University Press.

Webster's New World Dictionary. 1971. Cleveland: World Publishing.

Webster's New Collegiate Dictionary. 1975. Springfield, Massachusetts: Merriam.

Weinrich, Harald. 1964. Tempus: besprochene und Erzählte Welt. Stuttgart: W. Kohlhammer Verlag.

———. 1973. Le temps. tr. by Michèle Lacoste. Paris: Seuil.

———. 1982. Textgrammatik der französischen Sprache. Stuttgart: Klett.

———. 1989. Grammaire textuelle du français. (Version revue et corrigé de la Textgrammatik der französischen Sprache, tr. by Gilbert Dalgalian and Daniel Malbert.) Paris: Les Editions Didier.

Summer Institute of Linguistics and
The University of Texas at Arlington
Publications in Linguistics

10. **Verb studies in five New Guinea languages,** ed. by Alan Pence. 1964.
15. **Bolivian Indian tribes: Classification, bibliography and map of present language distribution,** by Harold Key and Mary R. Key. 1967.
18. **Tzotzil grammar,** by Marion M. Cowan. 1969.
19. **Aztec studies 1: Phonological and grammatical studies in modern Nahuatl dialects,** ed. by Dow F. Robinson. 1969.
20. **The phonology of Capanahua and its grammatical basis,** by Eugene E. Loos. 1969.
21. **Philippine languages: Discourse, paragraph and sentence structure,** by Robert E. Longacre. 1970.
22. **Aztec studies 2: Sierra Nahuat word structure,** by Dow F. Robinson. 1970.
23. **Tagmemic and matrix linguistics applied to selected African languages,** by Kenneth L. Pike. 1970.
24. **The grammar of Lamani,** by Ronald L. Trail. 1970.
25. **A linguistic sketch of Jicaltepec Mixtec,** by C. Henry Bradley. 1970.
26. **Major grammatical patterns of Western Bukidnon Manobo,** by Richard E. Elkins. 1970.
27. **Central Bontoc: Sentence, paragraph and discourse,** by Lawrence A. Reid. 1970.
28. **Identification of participants in discourse: A study of aspects of form and meaning in Nomatsiguenga,** by Mary Ruth Wise. 1971.
29. **Tupi studies 1,** ed. by David Bendor-Samuel. 1971.
30. **L'énoncé Toura (Côte d'Ivoire),** by Thomas Bearth. 1971.
33. **Two studies on the Lacandones of Mexico,** by Phillip Baer and William R. Merrifield. 1971.
36. **Tagmeme sequences in the English noun phrase,** by Peter H. Fries. 1970.
37. **Hierarchical structures in Guajajara,** by David Bendor-Samuel. 1972.
38. **Dialect intelligibility testing,** by Eugene H. Casad. 1974.
39. **Preliminary grammar of Auca,** by M. Catherine Peeke. 1973.
40.1. **Clause, sentence, and discourse patterns in selected languages of Nepal 1: General approach,** ed. by Austin Hale. 1973.
40.2. **Clause, sentence, and discourse patterns in selected languages of Nepal 2: Clause,** ed. by Austin Hale and David Watters. 1973.
40.3. **Clause, sentence, and discourse patterns in selected languages of Nepal 3: Texts,** ed. by Austin Hale. 1973.
40.4. **Clause, sentence, and discourse patterns in selected languages of Nepal 4: Word lists,** ed. by Austin Hale. 1973.
41.1. **Patterns in clause, sentence, and discourse in selected languages of India and Nepal 1: Sentence and discourse,** ed. by Ronald L. Trail. 1973.
41.2. **Patterns in clause, sentence, and discourse in selected languages of India and Nepal 2: Clause,** ed. by Ronald L. Trail. 1973.
41.3. **Patterns in clause, sentence, and discourse in selected languages of India and Nepal 3: Texts,** ed. by Ronald L. Trail. 1973.
41.4. **Patterns in clause, sentence, and discourse in selected languages of India and Nepal 4: Word lists,** ed. by Ronald L. Trail. 1973.

42. A generative syntax of Peñoles Mixtec, by John P. Daly. 1973.
43. Daga grammar: From morpheme to discourse, by Elizabeth Murane. 1974.
44. A hierarchical sketch of Mixe as spoken in San José El Paraíso, by Julia D. Van Haitsma and Willard Van Haitsma. 1976.
45. Network grammars, ed. by Joseph E. Grimes. 1975.
46. A description of Hiligaynon syntax, by Elmer Wolfenden. 1975.
47. A grammar of Izi, an Igbo language, by Paul E. Meier, Inge Meier, and John T. Bendor-Samuel. 1975.
48. Semantic relationships of Gahuku verbs, by Ellis W. Deibler. 1976.
49. Sememic and grammatical structures in Gurung, by Warren W. Glover. 1974.
50. Clause structure: Surface structure and deep structure roles, by Shin Ja Joo Hwang. 1975.
51. Papers on discourse, ed. by Joseph E. Grimes. 1978.
52.1. Discourse grammar: Studies in indigenous languages of Colombia, Panama, and Ecuador 1, ed. by Robert E. Longacre and Frances Woods. 1976.
52.2. Discourse grammar: Studies in indigenous languages of Colombia, Panama, and Ecuador 2, ed. by Robert E. Longacre and Frances Woods. 1977.
52.3. Discourse grammar: Studies in indigenous languages of Colombia, Panama, and Ecuador 3, ed. by Robert E. Longacre and Frances Woods. 1977.
53. Grammatical analysis, by Kenneth L. Pike and Evelyn G. Pike. 1977.
54. Studies in Otomanguean phonology, ed. by William R. Merrifield. 1977.
55. Two studies in Middle American comparative linguistics, by David Oltrogge and Calvin R. Rensch. 1977.
56.1. An overview of Uto-Aztecan grammar: Studies in Uto-Aztecan grammar 1, by Ronald W. Langacker. 1977.
56.2. Modern Aztec grammatical sketches: Studies in Uto-Aztecan grammar 2, ed. by Ronald W. Langacker. 1979.
56.3. Uto-Aztecan grammatical sketches: Studies in Uto-Aztecan grammar 3, ed. by Ronald W. Langacker. 1982.
56.4. Southern Uto-Aztecan grammatical sketches: Studies in Uto-Aztecan grammar 4, ed. by Ronald W. Langacker. 1984.
57. The deep structure of the sentence in Sara-Ngambay dialogues, including a description of phrase, clause, and paragraph, by James Edward Thayer. 1978.
58.1. Discourse studies in Mesoamerican languages 1: Discussion, ed. by Linda K. Jones. 1979.
58.2. Discourse studies in Mesoamerican languages 2: Texts, ed. by Linda K. Jones. 1979.
59. The functions of reported speech in discourse, by Mildred L. Larson. 1978.
60. A grammatical description of the Engenni language, by Elaine Thomas. 1978.
61. Predicate and argument in Rengao grammar, by Kenneth J. Gregerson. 1979.
62. Nung grammar, by Janice E. Saul and Nancy F. Wilson. 1980.
63. Discourse grammar in Gaᵃdang, by Michael R. Walrod. 1979.
64. A framework for discourse analysis, by Wilbur N. Pickering. 1980.
65. A generative grammar of Afar, by Loren F. Bliese. 1981.
66. Phonology and morphology of Axininca Campa, by David L. Payne. 1981.
67. Pragmatic aspects of English text structure, by Larry B. Jones. 1983.
68. Syntactic change and syntactic reconstruction: A tagmemic approach, by John R. Costello. 1983.

69. Affix positions and cooccurrences: The PARADIGM program, by Joseph E. Grimes. 1983.
70. Babine & Carrier phonology: A historically oriented study, by Gillian L. Story. 1984.
71. Workbook for historical linguistics, by Winfred P. Lehmann. 1984.
72. Senoufo phonology, discourse to syllable (a prosodic approach), by Elizabeth Mills. 1984.
73. Pragmatics in non-Western perspective, ed. by George Huttar and Kenneth J. Gregerson. 1986.
74. English phonetic transcription, by Charles-James N. Bailey. 1985.
75. Sentence initial devices, ed. by Joseph E. Grimes. 1986.
76. Hixkaryana and linguistic typology, by Desmond C. Derbyshire. 1985.
77. Discourse features of Korean narration, by Shin Ja Joo Hwang. 1987.
78. Tense/aspect and the development of auxiliaries in Kru languages, by Lynelle Marchese. 1986.
79. Modes in Dényá Discourse, by Samson Negbo Abangma. 1987.
80. Current trends and issues in Hispanic linguistics, ed. by Lenard Studerus. 1987.
81. Aspects of Western Subanon formal speech, by William C. Hall. 1987.
82. Dinka vowel system, by Job Malou. 1988.
83. Studies in the syntax of Mixtecan languages 1, ed. by C. Henry Bradley and Barbara E. Hollenbach. 1988.
84. Insights into Tagalog: Reduplication, infixation, and stress from nonlinear phonology, by Koleen M. French. 1988.
85. The verbal piece in Ebira, by John R. Adive. 1989.
86. Comparative Kadai: Linguistic studies beyond Tai, ed. by Jerold A. Edmondson and David B. Solnit. 1988.
87. An etymological dictionary of the Chinantec languages: Studies in Chinantec languages 1, by Calvin R. Rensch. 1989.
88. Lealao Chinantec syntax: Studies in Chinantec languages 2, by James E. Rupp. 1989.
89. Comaltepec Chinantec syntax: Studies in Chinantec languages 3, by Judi Lynn Anderson. 1989.
90. Studies in the syntax of Mixtecan languages 2, ed. by C. Henry Bradley and Barbara E. Hollenbach. 1990.
91. Language maintenance in Melanesia: Sociolinguistics and social networks in New Caledonia, by Stephen J. Schooling. 1990.
92. Comanche dictionary and grammar, ed. by Lila W. Robinson and James Armagost. 1990.
93. Development and diversity: Language variation across time and space (A Festschrift for Charles-James N. Bailey), ed. by Jerold A. Edmondson, Crawford Feagin, and Peter Mühlhäusler. 1990.
94. Ika syntax: Studies in the languages of Colombia 1, by Paul S. Frank. 1990.
95. Syllables, tone, and verb paradigms: Studies in Chinantec languages 4, ed. by William R. Merrifield and Calvin R. Rensch. 1990.
96. Survey on a shoestring: A manual for small-scale language surveys, by Frank Blair. 1990.
97. Can literacy lead to development? A case study in literacy, adult education, and economic development in India, by Uwe Gustafsson. 1991.

98. **The structure of Thai narrative,** by Somsonge Burusphat. 1991.
99. **Tense and Aspect in Eight Languages of Cameroon,** ed. by Stephen C. Anderson and Bernard Comrie. 1991.
100. **A reference grammar of Southeastern Tepehuan,** by Thomas L. Willett. 1991.
101. **Barasano syntax: Studies in the languages of Colombia 2,** by Wendell Jones and Paula Jones. 1991.
102. **Tone in five languages of Cameroon,** ed. by Stephen C. Anderson. 1991.
103. **An autosegmental approach to Shilluk phonology,** by Leoma G. Gilley. 1992.
104. **Sentence repetition testing for studies of community bilingualism,** by Carla F. Radloff. 1991.
105. **Studies in the syntax of Mixtecan languages 3,** ed. by C. Henry Bradley and Barbara E. Hollenbach. 1991.
106. **Tepetotutla Chinantec syntax: Studies in Chinantec languages 5,** by David Westley. 1991.
107. **Language in context: Essays for Robert E. Longacre,** ed. by Shin Ja J. Hwang and William R. Merrifield. 1992.
108. **Phonological studies in four languages of Maluku,** ed. by Donald A. Burquest and Wyn D. Laidig. 1992.
109. **Switch reference in Koasati discourse,** by David Rising. 1992.
110. **Windows on bilingualism,** by Eugene Casad. 1992.
111. **Studies in the syntax of Mixtecan Languages 4,** ed. by C. Henry Bradley and Barbara E. Hollenbach. 1992.
112. **Retuará syntax: Studies in the languages of Colombia 3,** by Clay Strom. 1992.
113. **A pragmatic analysis of Norwegian modal particles,** by Erik E. Andvik. 1992.
114. **Proto Witotoan,** by Ricard P. Aschmann. 1993.
115. **The function of verb prefixes in Southwestern Otomí,** by Henrietta Andrews. 1993.
116. **The French imparfait and passé simple in discourse,** by Sharon Rebecca Rand. 1993.

For further information or a catalog of SIL publications write to:

International Academic Bookstore
7500 W. Camp Wisdom Road
Dallas, TX 75236